SELECTED POEMS
OF
AMY LOWELL

SELECTED POEMS
OF
AMY LOWELL

EDITED BY

JOHN LIVINGSTON LOWES

BOSTON AND NEW YORK

HOUGHTON MIFFLIN COMPANY

The Riverside Press Cambridge

The Riverside Press
CAMBRIDGE · MASSACHUSETTS
PRINTED IN THE U.S.A.

PREFACE

AMY LOWELL's collected poems, including the translations, number more than six hundred and fifty titles, in eleven volumes. This volume is designed to make available within brief compass a selection from her most distinctive work. All eleven volumes are represented, as are all Miss Lowell's characteristic verse-forms. In two cases excerpts have been admitted; otherwise all the selections are complete. It has seemed best to group the poems in accordance with their more or less obvious kinship in theme or treatment, rather than to follow the order of publication. For reasons which need no comment the first and second poems have been chosen from the first and last published volumes respectively. For the rest, the selections move, in the main, from the centre of Miss Lowell's world toward its remote periphery:

> Lilac in me because I am New England,
> Because my roots are in it.
>
> So I start, but never rest
> North or South or East or West. . .·.
> Four-soul'd like the wind am I,
> Voyaging an endless sky.

CONTENTS

SELECTED POEMS
OF
AMY LOWELL

BEFORE THE ALTAR

Before the Altar, bowed, he stands
With empty hands;
Upon it perfumed offerings burn
Wreathing with smoke the sacrificial urn.
Not one of all these has he given,
No flame of his has leapt to Heaven
Firesouled, vermilion-hearted,
Forked, and darted,
Consuming what a few spare pence
Have cheaply bought, to fling from hence
In idly-asked petition.

His sole condition
Love and poverty.
And while the moon
Swings slow across the sky,
Athwart a waving pine tree
And soon
Tips all the needles there
With silver sparkles, bitterly
He gazes, while his soul
Grows hard with thinking of the poorness of
      his dole.

"Shining and distant Goddess, hear my prayer
  Where you swim in the high air!
  With charity look down on me,
  Under this tree,
  Tending the gifts I have not brought,
  The rare and goodly things
  I have not sought.
  Instead, take from me all my life!

'Upon the wings
  Of shimmering moonbeams
  I pack my poet's dreams
  For you.
  My wearying strife,
  My courage, my loss,
  Into the night I toss
  For you.
  Golden Divinity,
  Deign to look down on me
  Who so unworthily
  Offers to you:
  All life has known,
  Seeds withered unsown,
  Hopes turning quick to fears,
  Laughter which dies in tears.
  The shredded remnant of a man
  Is all the span

And compass of my offering to you.

"Empty and silent, I
Kneel before your pure, calm majesty.
On this stone, in this urn
I pour my heart and watch it burn,
Myself the sacrifice; but be
Still unmoved: Divinity."

From the altar, bathed in moonlight,
The smoke rose straight in the quiet night.

SHOOTING THE SUN

FOUR horizons cozen me
To distances I dimly see.
Four paths beckon me to stray,
Each a bold and separate way.
Monday morning shows the East
Satisfying as a feast.
Tuesday I will none of it,
West alone holds benefit.
Later in the week 'tis due
North that I would hurry to.
While on other days I find
To the South content of mind.
So I start, but never rest
North or South or East or West.
Each horizon has its claim
Solace to a different aim.
Four-soul'd like the wind am I,
Voyaging an endless sky,
Undergoing destiny.

MEETING-HOUSE HILL

I MUST be mad, or very tired,
When the curve of a blue bay beyond a railroad track
Is shrill and sweet to me like the sudden springing of a
       tune,
And the sight of a white church above thin trees in a city
       square
Amazes my eyes as though it were the Parthenon.
Clear, reticent, superbly final,
With the pillars of its portico refined to a cautious ele-
       gance,
It dominates the weak trees,
And the shot of its spire
Is cool, and candid,
Rising into an unresisting sky.
Strange meeting-house
Pausing a moment upon a squalid hill-top.
I watch the spire sweeping the sky,
I am dizzy with the movement of the sky,
I might be watching a mast
With its royals set full
Straining before a two-reef breeze.
I might be sighting a tea-clipper,
Tacking into the blue bay,

Just back from Canton
With her hold full of green and blue porcelain,
And a Chinese coolie leaning over the rail
Gazing at the white spire
With dull, sea-spent eyes.

ST. LOUIS

JUNE

FLAT,
Flat,
Long as sight
Either way.
An immense country,
With a great river
Steaming it full of moist, unbearable heat.
The orchards are little quincunxes of Noah's Ark trees,
The plows and horses are children's toys tracing amus-
      ingly shallow lines upon an illimitable surface.
Great chunks of life to match the country,
Great lungs to breathe this hot, wet air.

But it is not mine.
Mine is a land of hills
Lying couchant in the angles of heraldic beasts
About white villages.
A land of singing elms and pine-trees.
A restless up and down land
Always mounting, dipping, slipping into a different con-
      tour,
Where the roads turn every hundred yards or so,

Where brooks rattle forgotten Indian names to tired
    farm-houses,
And faint spires of old meeting-houses
Flaunt their golden weather-cocks in a brave show of
    challenge at a sunset sky.

Here the heat stuffs down with the thickness of boiled
    feathers,
The river runs in steam.
There, lilacs are in bloom,
Cool blue-purples, wine-reds, whites,
Flying colour to quiet dooryards.
Grown year on year to a suddenness of old perfection,
Saying, "Before! Before!" to each new Spring.
Here is "Now,"
But "Before" is mine with the lilacs,
With the white sea of everywhither,
With the heraldic, story-telling hills.

LILACS

Lilacs,
False blue,
White,
Purple,
Colour of lilac,
Your great puffs of flowers
Are everywhere in this my New England.
Among your heart-shaped leaves
Orange orioles hop like music-box birds and sing
Their little weak soft songs;
In the crooks of your branches
The bright eyes of song sparrows sitting on spotted
     eggs
Peer restlessly through the light and shadow
Of all Springs.
Lilacs in dooryards
Holding quiet conversations with an early moon;
Lilacs watching a deserted house
Settling sideways into the grass of an old road;
Lilacs, wind-beaten, staggering under a lopsided shock
     of bloom
Above a cellar dug into a hill.
You are everywhere.

You were everywhere.

You tapped the window when the preacher preached his
      sermon,

And ran along the road beside the boy going to school.

You stood by pasture-bars to give the cows good milk-
      ing,

You persuaded the housewife that her dish pan was of
      silver

And her husband an image of pure gold.

You flaunted the fragrance of your blossoms

Through the wide doors of Custom Houses —

You, and sandal-wood, and tea,

Charging the noses of quill-driving clerks

When a ship was in from China.

You called to them: "Goose-quill men, goose-quill men,

May is a month for flitting,"

Until they writhed on their high stools

And wrote poetry on their letter-sheets behind the
      propped-up ledgers.

Paradoxical New England clerks,

Writing inventories in ledgers, reading the "Song of
      Solomon" at night,

So many verses before bed-time,

Because it was the Bible.

The dead fed you

Amid the slant stones of graveyards.

Pale ghosts who planted you

Came in the night-time

And let their thin hair blow through your clustered
    stems.
You are of the green sea,
And of the stone hills which reach a long distance.
You are of elm-shaded streets with little shops where
    they sell kites and marbles,
You are of great parks where everyone walks and no-
    body is at home.
You cover the blind sides of greenhouses
And lean over the top to say a hurry-word through the
    glass
To your friends, the grapes, inside.

Lilacs,
False blue,
White,
Purple,
Colour of lilac,
You have forgotten your Eastern origin,
The veiled women with eyes like panthers,
The swollen, aggressive turbans of jewelled Pashas.
Now you are a very decent flower,
A reticent flower,
A curiously clear-cut, candid flower,
Standing beside clean doorways,
Friendly to a house-cat and a pair of spectacles,
Making poetry out of a bit of moonlight
And a hundred or two sharp blossoms.

Maine knows you,
Has for years and years;
New Hampshire knows you,
And Massachusetts
And Vermont.
Cape Cod starts you along the beaches to Rhode Island;
Connecticut takes you from a river to the sea.
You are brighter than apples,
Sweeter than tulips,
You are the great flood of our souls
Bursting above the leaf-shapes of our hearts,
You are the smell of all Summers,
The love of wives and children,
The recollection of the gardens of little children,
You are State Houses and Charters
And the familiar treading of the foot to and fro on a road
    it knows.
May is lilac here in New England,
May is a thrush singing "Sun up!" on a tip-top ash-tree,
May is white clouds behind pine-trees
Puffed out and marching upon a blue sky.
May is a green as no other,
May is much sun through small leaves,
May is soft earth,
And apple-blossoms,
And windows open to a South wind.
May is a full light wind of lilac

From Canada to Narragansett Bay.

Lilacs,
False blue,
White,
Purple,
Colour of lilac.
Heart-leaves of lilac all over New England,
Roots of lilac under all the soil of New England,
Lilac in me because I am New England,
Because my roots are in it,
Because my leaves are of it,
Because my flowers are for it,
Because it is my country
And I speak to it of itself
And sing of it with my own voice
Since certainly it is mine.

PURPLE GRACKLES

THE grackles have come.
The smoothness of the morning is puckered with their
　　　incessant chatter.
A sociable lot, these purple grackles,
Thousands of them strung across a long run of wind,
Thousands of them beating the air-ways with quick
　　　wing-jerks,
Spinning down the currents of the South.
Every year they come,
My garden is a place of solace and recreation evidently,
For they always pass a day with me.
With high good nature they tell me what I do not want
　　　to hear.
The grackles have come.

I am persuaded that grackles are birds;
But when they are settled in the trees,
I am inclined to declare them fruits
And the trees turned hybrid blackberry vines.
Blackness shining and bulging under leaves,
Does not that mean blackberries, I ask you?
Nonsense! The grackles have come.

Nonchalant highwaymen, pickpockets, second-story
      burglars,
Stealing away my little hope of Summer.
There is no stealthy robbing in this.
Who ever heard such a gabble of thieves' talk!
It seems they delight in unmasking my poor pre-
      tence.
Yes, now I see that the hydrangea blooms are rusty;
That the hearts of the golden glow are ripening to
      lustreless seeds;
That the garden is dahlia-coloured,
Flaming with its last over-hot hues;
That the sun is pale as a lemon too small to fill the
      picking-ring.
I did not see this yesterday,
But to-day the grackles have come.

They drop out of the trees
And strut in companies over the lawn,
Tired of flying, no doubt;
A grand parade to limber legs and give wings a rest.
I should build a great fish-pond for them,
Since it is evident that a bird-bath, meant to accom-
      modate two goldfinches at most,
Is slight hospitality for these hordes.
Scarcely one can get in,
They all peck and scrabble so,

Crowding, pushing, chasing one another up the bank
    with spread wings.

"Are we ducks, you, owner of such inadequate com-
    forts,

That you offer us lily-tanks where one must swim or
    drown,

Not stand and splash like a gentleman?"

I feel the reproach keenly, seeing them perch on the
    edges of the tanks, trying the depth with a
    chary foot,

And hardly able to get their wings under water in the
    bird-bath.

But there are resources I had not considered,

If I am bravely ruled out of count.

What is that thudding against the eaves just beyond
    my window?

What is that spray of water blowing past my face?

Two — three — grackles bathing in the gutter,

The gutter providentially choked with leaves.

I pray they think I put the leaves there on purpose;

I would be supposed thoughtful and welcoming

To all guests, even thieves.

But considering that they are going South and I am
    not,

I wish they would bathe more quietly,

It is unmannerly to flaunt one's good fortune.

They rate me of no consequence,

But they might reflect that it is my gutter.
I know their opinion of me,
Because one is drying himself on the window-sill
Not two feet from my hand.
His purple neck is sleek with water,
And the fellow preens his feathers for all the world as
    if I were a fountain statue.
If it were not for the window,
I am convinced he would light on my head.
Tyrian-feathered freebooter,
Appropriating my delightful gutter with so extravagant
    an ease,
You are as cool a pirate as ever scuttled a ship,
And are you not scuttling my Summer with every peck
    of your sharp bill?

But there is a cloud over the beech-tree,
A quenching cloud for lemon-livered suns.
The grackles are all swinging in the tree-tops,
And the wind is coming up, mind you.
That boom and reach is no Summer gale,
I know that wind,
It blows the Equinox over seeds and scatters them,
It rips petals from petals, and tears off half-turned
    leaves.
There is rain on the back of that wind.
Now I would keep the grackles,
I would plead with them not to leave me.

I grant their coming, but I would not have them go.
It is a milestone, this passing of grackles.
A day of them, and it is a year gone by.
There is magic in this and terror,
But I only stare stupidly out of the window.
The grackles have come.

Come! Yes, they surely came.
But they have gone.
A moment ago the oak was full of them,
They are not there now.
Not a speck of a black wing,
Not an eye-peep of a purple head.
The grackles have gone,
And I watch an Autumn storm
Stripping the garden,
Shouting black rain challenges
To an old, limp Summer
Laid down to die in the flower-beds.

THE CORNER OF NIGHT AND MORNING

CROWS are cawing over pine-trees,
They are teaching their young to fly
Above the tall pyramids of double cherries.
Rose lustre over black lacquer —
The feathers of the young birds reflect the rose-rising
     sun.
Caw! Caw!
I want to go to sleep,
But perhaps it is better to stand in the window
And watch the crows teaching their young to fly
Over the pines and the pyramidal cherries,
In the rose-gold light
Of five o'clock on a May morning.

DAWN ADVENTURE

I STOOD in my window
>> looking at the double cherry:
A great height of white stillness,
Underneath a sky
>> the colour of milky grey jade.
Suddenly a crow flew between me and the tree —
Swooping, falling, in a shadow-black curve —
And blotted himself out in the blurred branches of a
>> leafless ash.
There he stayed for some time,
>> and I could only distinguish him by his slight
>>>> moving.
Then a wind caught the upper branches of the cherry,
And the long, white stems nodded up and down, casually,
>> to me in the window,
Nodded — but overhead the grey jade clouds
>> passed slowly, indifferently, toward the sea.

BEECH, PINE, AND SUNLIGHT

THE sudden April heat
Stretches itself
Under the smooth, leafless branches
Of the beech-tree,
And lies lightly
Upon the great patches
Of purple and white crocus
With their panting, wide-open cups.

A clear wind
Slips through the naked beech boughs,
And their shadows scarcely stir.
But the pine-trees beyond sigh
When it passes over them
And presses back their needles,
And slides gently down their stems.

It is a languor of pale, south-starting sunlight
Come upon a morning unawaked,
And holding her drowsing.

DOG–DAYS

A LADDER sticking up at the open window,
The top of an old ladder;
And all of Summer is there.

Great waves and tufts of wistaria surge across the
window,
And a thin, belated blossom
Jerks up and down in the sunlight;
Purple translucence against the blue sky.
"Tie back this branch," I say,
But my hands are sticky with leaves,
And my nostrils widen to the smell of crushed green.
The ladder moves uneasily at the open window,
And I call to the man beneath,
"Tie back that branch."

There is a ladder leaning against the window-sill,
And a mutter of thunder in the air.

THE GARDEN BY MOONLIGHT

A BLACK cat among roses,
Phlox, lilac-misted under a first-quarter moon,
The sweet smells of heliotrope and night-scented stock.
The garden is very still,
It is dazed with moonlight,
Contented with perfume,
Dreaming the opium dreams of its folded poppies.
Firefly lights open and vanish
High as the tip buds of the golden glow
Low as the sweet alyssum flowers at my feet.
Moon-shimmer on leaves and trellises,
Moon-spikes shafting through the snow-ball bush.
Only the little faces of the ladies' delight are alert and
          staring,
Only the cat, padding between the roses,
Shakes a branch and breaks the chequered pattern
As water is broken by the falling of a leaf.
Then you come,
And you are quiet like the garden,
And white like the alyssum flowers,
And beautiful as the silent sparks of the fireflies.
Ah, Beloved, do you see those orange lilies?
They knew my mother,
But who belonging to me will they know
When I am gone.

SUMMER NIGHT PIECE

THE garden is steeped in moonlight,
Full to its high edges with brimming silver,
And the fish-ponds brim and darken
And run in little serpent lights soon extinguished.
Lily-pads lie upon the surface, beautiful as the tarnish-
        ings on frail old silver,
And the Harvest moon droops heavily out of the sky,
A ripe, white melon, intensely, magnificently, shining.
Your window is orange in the moonlight,
It glows like a lamp behind the branches of the old
        wistaria,
It burns like a lamp before a shrine,
The small, intimate, familiar shrine
Placed reverently among the bricks
Of a much-loved garden wall.

BEHIND A WALL

I OWN a solace shut within my heart,
  A garden full of many a quaint delight
  And warm with drowsy, poppied sunshine; bright,
Flaming with lilies out of whose cups dart
    Shining things
    With powdered wings.

Here terrace sinks to terrace, arbors close
  The ends of dreaming paths; a wanton wind
  Jostles the half-ripe pears, and then, unkind,
Tumbles a-slumber in a pillar rose,
    With content
    Grown indolent.

By night my garden is o'erhung with gems
  Fixed in an onyx setting. Fireflies
  Flicker their lanterns in my dazzled eyes.
In serried rows I guess the straight, stiff stems
    Of hollyhocks
    Against the rocks.

So far and still it is that, listening,
  I hear the flowers talking in the dawn;

And where a sunken basin cuts the lawn,
Cinctured with iris, pale and glistening,
The sudden swish
Of a waking fish.

JULY MIDNIGHT

FIREFLIES flicker in the tops of trees
Flicker in the lower branches,
Skim along the ground.
Over the moon-white lilies
Is a flashing and ceasing of small, lemon-green stars.
As you lean against me,
Moon-white,
The air all about you
Is slit, and pricked, and pointed with sparkles of lemon-
    green flame
Starting out of a background of vague, blue trees.

BRIGHT SUNLIGHT

THE wind has blown a corner of your shawl
Into the fountain,
Where it floats and drifts
Among the lily-pads
Like a tissue of sapphires.
But you do not heed it,
Your fingers pick at the lichens
On the stone edge of the basin,
And your eyes follow the tall clouds
As they sail over the ilex-trees.

VENUS TRANSIENS

TELL me,
Was Venus more beautiful
Than you are,
When she topped
The crinkled waves,
Drifting shoreward
On her plaited shell?
Was Botticelli's vision
Fairer than mine;
And were the painted rosebuds
He tossed his lady,
Of better worth
Than the words I blow about you
To cover your too great loveliness
As with a gauze
Of misted silver?

For me,
You stand poised
In the blue and buoyant air,
Cinctured by bright winds,
Treading the sunlight.
And the waves which precede you
Ripple and stir
The sands at my feet.

MADONNA OF THE EVENING FLOWERS

ALL day long I have been working,
Now I am tired.
I call: "Where are you?"
But there is only the oak-tree rustling in the wind.
The house is very quiet,
The sun shines in on your books,
On your scissors and thimble just put down,
But you are not there.
Suddenly I am lonely:
Where are you?
I go about searching.

Then I see you,
Standing under a spire of pale blue larkspur,
With a basket of roses on your arm.
You are cool, like silver,
And you smile.
I think the Canterbury bells are playing little
          tunes.

You tell me that the peonies need spraying,
That the columbines have overrun all bounds,

That the pyrus japonica should be cut back and
    rounded.
You tell me these things.
But I look at you, heart of silver,
White heart-flame of polished silver,
Burning beneath the blue steeples of the larkspur,
And I long to kneel instantly at your feet,
While all about us peal the loud, sweet *Te Deums*
    of the Canterbury bells.

A SPRIG OF ROSEMARY

I CANNOT see your face.
When I think of you,
It is your hands which I see.
Your hands
Sewing,
Holding a book,
Resting for a moment on the sill of a window.
My eyes keep always the sight of your hands,
But my heart holds the sound of your voice,
And the soft brightness which is your soul.

NOSTALGIA

"THROUGH pleasures and palaces" —
Through hotels, and Pullman cars, and steamships . . .

Pink and white camellias
       floating in a crystal bowl,
The sharp smell of firewood,
The scrape and rustle of a dog stretching himself
       on a hardwood floor,
And your voice, reading — reading —
       to the slow ticking of an old brass clock . . .

"Tickets, please!"
And I watch the man in front of me
Fumbling in fourteen pockets,
While the conductor balances his ticket-punch
Between his fingers.

THE FRUIT GARDEN PATH

THE path runs straight between the flowering rows,
  A moonlit path, hemmed in by beds of bloom,
  Where phlox and marigolds dispute for room
With tall, red dahlias and the briar rose.
'Tis reckless prodigality which throws
  Into the night these wafts of rich perfume
  Which sweep across the garden like a plume.
Over the trees a single bright star glows.
  Dear garden of my childhood, here my years
Have run away like little grains of sand;
  The moments of my life, its hopes and fears
Have all found utterance here, where now I stand;
  My eyes ache with the weight of unshed tears,
You are my home, do you not understand?

GARDEN GAMES

(From "A Roxbury Garden")

THE tall clock is striking twelve;
And the little girls stop in the hall to watch it,
And the big ships rocking in a half-circle
Above the dial.
Twelve o'clock!
Down the side steps
Go the little girls,
Under their big round straw hats.
Minna's has a pink ribbon,
Stella's a blue,
That is the way they know which is which.
Twelve o'clock!
An hour yet before dinner.
Mother is busy in the still-room,
And Hannah is making gingerbread.
Slowly, with lagging steps,
They follow the garden-path,
Crushing a leaf of box for its acrid smell,
Discussing what they shall do,
And doing nothing.

"Stella, see that grasshopper
Climbing up the bank!

What a jump!
Almost as long as my arm."
Run, children, run.
For the grasshopper is leaping away,
In half-circle curves,
Shuttlecock curves,
Over the grasses.
Hand in hand, the little girls call to him:
  "Grandfather, grandfather gray,
    Give me molasses, or I'll throw you away."
The grasshopper leaps into the sunlight,
Golden-green,
And is gone.

"Let's catch a bee."
Round whirl the little girls,
And up the garden.
Two heads are thrust among the Canterbury bells,
Listening,
And fingers clasp and unclasp behind backs
In a strain of silence.

White bells,
Blue bells,
Hollow and reflexed.
Deep tunnels of blue and white dimness,
Cool wine-tunnels for bees.
There is a floundering and buzzing over Minna's head.

"Bend it down, Stella. Quick! Quick!"
The wide mouth of a blossom
Is pressed together in Minna's fingers.
The stem flies up, jiggling its flower-bells,
And Minna holds the dark blue cup in her hand,
With the bee
Imprisoned in it.
Whirr! Buzz! Bump!
Bump! Whiz! Bang!
BANG!!
The blue flower tears across like paper,
And a gold-black bee darts away in the sunshine.

"If we could fly, we could catch him."
The sunshine is hot on Stella's upturned face,
As she stares after the bee.
"We'll follow him in a dove chariot.
Come on, Stella."
Run, children,
Along the red gravel paths,
For a bee is hard to catch,
Even with a chariot of doves.

Tall, still, and cowled,
Stand the monk's-hoods;
Taller than the heads of the little girls.
A blossom for Minna.
A blossom for Stella.

Off comes the cowl,
And there is a purple-painted chariot;
Off comes the forward petal,
And there are two little green doves,
With green traces tying them to the chariot.
"Now we will get in, and fly right up to the clouds.
    Fly, Doves, up in the sky,
    With Minna and me,
    After the bee."

Up one path,
Down another,
Run the little girls,
Holding their dove chariots in front of them;
But the bee is hidden in the trumpet of a honeysuckle,
With his wings folded along his back.

The dove chariots are thrown away,
And the little girls wander slowly through the garden,
Sucking the salvia tips,
And squeezing the snapdragons
To make them gape.
"I'm so hot,
Let's pick a pansy
And see the little man in his bath,
And play we're he."
A royal bath-tub,
Hung with purple stuffs and yellow.

The great purple-yellow wings
Rise up behind the little red and green man;
The purple-yellow wings fan him,
He dabbles his feet in cool green.
Off with the green sheath,
And there are two spindly legs.
"Heigho!" sighs Minna.
"Heigho!" sighs Stella.
There is not a flutter of wind,
And the sun is directly overhead.

Along the edge of the garden
Walk the little girls.
Their hats, round and yellow like cheeses,
Are dangling by the ribbons.
The grass is a tumult of buttercups and daisies;
Buttercups and daisies streaming away
Up the hill.
The garden is purple, and pink, and orange, and scarlet;
The garden is hot with colours.
But the meadow is only yellow, and white, and green,
Cool, and long, and quiet.
The little girls pick buttercups
And hold them under each other's chins.
"You're as gold as Grandfather's snuff-box.
You're going to be very rich, Minna."
"Oh-o-o! Then I'll ask my husband to give me a pair of
        garnet earrings

Just like Aunt Nancy's.
I wonder if he will.
I know. We'll tell fortunes.
That's what we'll do."
Plump down in the meadow grass,
Stella and Minna,
With their round yellow hats,
Like cheeses,
Beside them.
Drop,
Drop,
Daisy petals.
    "One I love,
      Two I love,
      Three I love I say . . ."
The ground is peppered with daisy petals,
And the little girls nibble the golden centres,
And play it is cake.

A bell rings.
Dinner-time;
And after dinner there are lessons.

TRADES

I WANT to be a carpenter,
To work all day long in clean wood,
Shaving it into little thin slivers
Which screw up into curls behind my plane;
Pounding square, black nails into white boards,
With the claws of my hammer glistening
Like the tongue of a snake.
I want to shingle a house,
Sitting on the ridge-pole in a bright breeze.
I want to put the shingles on neatly,
Taking great care that each is directly between two
        others.
I want my hands to have the tang of wood:
Spruce, Cedar, Cypress.
I want to draw a line on a board with a flat pencil,
And then saw along that line,
With the sweet-smelling sawdust piling up in a yellow
        heap at my feet.

That is the life!
Heigh-ho!
It is much easier than to write this poem.

FROM A CRITICAL FABLE

"My dear Sir," I exclaimed, "if you'd not been afraid
Of Margaret Fuller's success, you'd have stayed
Your hand in her case and more justly have rated her."
Here he murmured morosely, "My God, how I hated
        her!
But have you no women whom you must hate too?
I shall think all the better of you if you do,
And of them, I may add." I assured him, "A few.
But I scarcely think man feels the same contradictory
Desire to love them and shear them of victory?"
"You think wrong, my young friend," he declared with
        a frown,
"Man will always love woman and always pull down
What she does." "Well, of course, if you will hug the
        cynical,
It is quite your affair, but there is the pinnacle.
She's welcome to climb with man if she wishes."
"And fall with a crash like a trayful of dishes,"
He answered at once, "but if there's no gainsaying her,
There's certainly not the least use in delaying her."
"Very well," I assured him, and quite without mockery,
"But I know several women not yet broken crockery.
Amy Lowell, for instance," I spoke a bit clammily.

"Good Heavens!" he shouted, "not one of the family!
I remember they used to be counted by dozens,
But I never was interested in immature cousins."
"They grow, I believe." The retort was so pat
There was nothing to say, and he pulled down his hat.
I continued: "But since this is not genealogy,
You'll permit me to waive any sort of analogy
Between her and your friend. No one likes to be
        bound
In a sort of perpetual family pound
Tied by *esprit de corps* to the wheels of the dead.
A poet above all people must have his head.
Indeed it's been whispered the lady sees red
When the subject is broached, she will find her own
        latitude."
"My friend, were he here, would extol such an atti-
        tude,"
He said very gravely. "But proceed, Sir, I pray."
I hastened as fast as I could to obey:
"Conceive, if you can, an electrical storm
Of a swiftness and fury surpassing the norm;
Conceive that this cyclone has caught up the rainbow
And dashed dizzily on with it streaming in tow.
Imagine a sky all split open and scissored
By lightnings, and then you can picture this blizzard.
That is, if you'll also imagine the clashes
Of tropical thunder, the incessant crashes
Which shiver the hearing and leave it in ashes.

Remember, meanwhile, that the sky is prismatic
And outrageous with colour. The effect is erratic
And jarring to some, but to others ecstatic,
Depending, of course, on the idiosyncratic
Response of beholders. When you come to think of it,
A good deal is demanded by those on the brink of it.
To be caught in the skirts of a whirling afflatus
One must not suppose is experienced gratis.
Broncho-busting with rainbows is scarcely a game
For middle-aged persons inclined to the tame.
Likewise, who'd enjoy a sunrise from the Matter-
horn — something all travellers agree is the attar
Of distilled perfection — must be ready to reap
The mid-afternoon pangs of too little sleep.
I might go on forever commingling my metaphors,
And verse by this means does undoubtedly get a force,
But persons who so air their fancy are bores,
A thing every bone in my body abhors,
And you'll guess by this time, without farther allusion,
That the lady's unique and surprising profusion
Creates in some minds an unhappy confusion.
No one's to be blamed who's not something and
        twenty,
But it's lucky for her that young folk are so plenty.
The future's her goose and I dare say she'll wing it,
Though the triumph will need her own power to sing it.
Although I'm no prophet, I'll hazard a guess
She'll be rated by time as more rather than less.

Once accustom yourself to her strange elocution,
And milder verse seems by contrast mere dilution.
Then again (for I've kept back a very great part),
Despite her traducers, there's always a heart
Hid away in her poems for the seeking; impassioned,
Beneath silver surfaces cunningly fashioned
To baffle coarse pryings, it waits for the touch
Of a man who takes surfaces only as such.
Her work's not, if you will, for the glib amateur,
But I wonder, would it be improved if it were?
Must subtlety always be counted a flaw
And poetry not poetry which puzzles the raw?
Let me turn for an instant to note the reverse
Of my poet, who employs many manners of verse
And when not hurricaning's astoundingly terse;
Yet here the poor creature but makes matters worse.
There are plenty of critics who say they can't hear
When she sings *sotto voce*, the sensation's queer
And inspires a species of horrible fear.
To be told there's a sound and catch nothing at all,
Is a circumstance fairly designed to appal
Most casual people, for here is the hitch:
The admission that one's own ears can't grasp a pitch
Clear and lovely to others. Whereupon a bow-wow
Which swells to a perfectly hideous row.
They've accused her of every description of quackery,
Of only concerning herself with knick-knackery,
It has all been enough to set any one's back awry.

She's a fool to resent it, a man would have grinned?
Quite so, but then poets are created thin-skinned,
And when one is more than a little volcanic,
With a very strong dash of the ultra-tyrannic,
The retort contentious will be simply Titanic.
Behold, then, our poet, by the lash of atrociousness
Goaded into an attitude much like ferociousness.
Every book that she writes has a preface to guard it
Which spits fire and cannon-balls, making each hard hit
Tell, and mow down its swathe of objectors.
But critics have ever been good resurrectors.
Since she keeps the fight going, they rise to do battle,
When the whole mess is only so much tittle-tattle.
So it goes back and forth with the cries and the cheer-
        ing,
And there's no sign at all of the atmosphere clearing.
Her books follow each other despite all the riot,
For, oddly enough, there's a queer, crumpled quiet
Perpetually round her, a crazy-quilt tent
Dividing her happily from the event.
Armed to the teeth like an old Samurai,
Juggling with jewels like the ancient genii,
Hung all over with mouse-traps of metres, and cages
Of bright-plumaged rhythms, with pages and pages
Of colours slit up into streaming confetti
Which give the appearance of something sunsetty,
And gorgeous, and flowing — a curious sight
She makes in her progress, a modern White Knight,

Forever explaining her latest inventions
And assuring herself of all wandering attentions
By pausing at times to sing, in a duly
Appreciative manner, an aria from Lully.
The horse which she rides will suit any part
Either Peg (with the 'asus,') or 'Peg o' my heart.'
To avoid making blunders, he's usually known
Without any suffix as 'Peg' all alone.
This style of address has become a tradition
Most offendingly silly, since no erudition
Unaided can ever produce a magician.
For the magic she has, I see nothing demonic
In the use of free verse (the 'free' is quite comic!)
Or even that mule of the arts, polyphonic.
No matter what pedants may find that's awry in him,
There's plenty of kick and plenty of fly in him.
Taking this thing and that, and considering on it,
I believe there are more guesses under her bonnet
Than in any two hats you are likely to meet
(Straw or felt, take your choice, so the shape be discreet,
Not too flap-brimmed and weird, nor too jaunty and
          neat)
In any particular city or street
You may happen to pick."

THE SISTERS

TAKING us by and large, we're a queer lot
We women who write poetry. And when you think
How few of us there've been, it's queerer still.
I wonder what it is that makes us do it,
Singles us out to scribble down, man-wise,
The fragments of ourselves. Why are we
Already mother-creatures, double-bearing,
With matrices in body and in brain?
I rather think that there is just the reason
We are so sparse a kind of human being;
The strength of forty thousand Atlases
Is needed for our every-day concerns.
There's Sapho, now I wonder what was Sapho.
I know a single slender thing about her:
That, loving, she was like a burning birch-tree
All tall and glittering fire, and that she wrote
Like the same fire caught up to Heaven and held there,
A frozen blaze before it broke and fell.
Ah, me! I wish I could have talked to Sapho,
Surprised her reticences by flinging mine
Into the wind. This tossing off of garments
Which cloud the soul is none too easy doing
With us to-day. But still I think with Sapho

One might accomplish it, were she in the mood
To bare her loveliness of words and tell
The reasons, as she possibly conceived them,
Of why they are so lovely. Just to know
How she came at them, just to watch
The crisp sea sunshine playing on her hair,
And listen, thinking all the while 'twas she
Who spoke and that we two were sisters
Of a strange, isolated little family.
And she is Sapho — Sapho — not Miss or Mrs.,
A leaping fire we call so for convenience;
But Mrs. Browning — who would ever think
Of such presumption as to call her "Ba."
Which draws the perfect line between sea-cliffs
And a close-shuttered room in Wimpole Street.
Sapho could fly her impulses like bright
Balloons tip-tilting to a morning air
And write about it. Mrs. Browning's heart
Was squeezed in stiff conventions. So she lay
Stretched out upon a sofa, reading Greek
And speculating, as I must suppose,
In just this way on Sapho; all the need,
The huge, imperious need of loving, crushed
Within the body she believed so sick.
And it was sick, poor lady, because words
Are merely simulacra after deeds
Have wrought a pattern; when they take the place
Of actions they breed a poisonous miasma

Which, though it leave the brain, eats up the body.
So Mrs. Browning, aloof and delicate,
Lay still upon her sofa, all her strength
Going to uphold her over-topping brain.
It seems miraculous, but she escaped
To freedom and another motherhood
Than that of poems. She was a very woman
And needed both.

     If I had gone to call,
Would Wimpole Street have been the kindlier place,
Or Casa Guidi, in which to have met her?
I am a little doubtful of that meeting,
For Queen Victoria was very young and strong
And all-pervading in her apogee
At just that time. If we had stuck to poetry,
Sternly refusing to be drawn off by mesmerism
Or Roman revolutions, it might have done.
For, after all, she is another sister,
But always, I rather think, an older sister
And not herself so curious a technician
As to admit newfangled modes of writing —
"Except, of course, in Robert, and that is neither
Here nor there for Robert is a genius."
I do not like the turn this dream is taking,
Since I am very fond of Mrs. Browning
And very much indeed should like to hear her
Graciously asking me to call her "Ba."
But then the Devil of Verisimilitude

Creeps in and forces me to know she wouldn't.
Convention again, and how it chafes my nerves,
For we are such a little family
Of singing sisters, and as if I didn't know
What those years felt like tied down to the sofa.
Confound Victoria, and the slimy inhibitions
She loosed on all us Anglo-Saxon creatures!
Suppose there hadn't been a Robert Browning,
No "Sonnets from the Portuguese" would have been
      written.
They are the first of all her poems to be,
One might say, fertilized. For, after all,
A poet is flesh and blood as well as brain
And Mrs. Browning, as I said before,
Was very, very woman. Well, there are two
Of us, and vastly unlike that's for certain.
Unlike at least until we tear the veils
Away which commonly gird souls. I scarcely think
Mrs. Browning would have approved the process
In spite of what had surely been relief;
For speaking souls must always want to speak
Even when bat-eyed, narrow-minded Queens
Set prudishness to keep the keys of impulse.
Then do the frowning Gods invent new banes
And make the need of sofas. But Sapho was dead
And I, and others, not yet peeped above
The edge of possibility. So that's an end
To speculating over tea-time talks

Beyond the movement of pentameters
With Mrs. Browning.

                    But I go dreaming on,
In love with these my spiritual relations.
I rather think I see myself walk up
A flight of wooden steps and ring a bell
And send a card in to Miss Dickinson.
Yet that's a very silly way to do.
I should have taken the dream twist-ends about
And climbed over the fence and found her deep
Engrossed in the doings of a humming-bird
Among nasturtiums. Not having expected strangers,
She might forget to think me one, and holding up
A finger say quite casually: "Take care.
Don't frighten him, he's only just begun."
"Now this," I well believe I should have thought,
"Is even better than Sapho. With Emily
You're really here, or never anywhere at all
In range of mind." Wherefore, having begun
In the strict centre, we could slowly progress
To various circumferences, as we pleased.
We could, but should we? That would quite depend
On Emily. I think she'd be exacting,
Without intention possibly, and ask
A thousand tight-rope tricks of understanding.
But, bless you, I would somersault all day
If by so doing I might stay with her.
I hardly think that we should mention souls

Although they might just round the corner from us
In some half-quizzical, half-wistful metaphor.
I'm very sure that I should never seek
To turn her parables to stated fact.
Sapho would speak, I think, quite openly,
And Mrs. Browning guard a careful silence,
But Emily would set doors ajar and slam them
And love you for your speed of observation.

Strange trio of my sisters, most diverse,
And how extraordinarily unlike
Each is to me, and which way shall I go?
Sapho spent and gained; and Mrs. Browning,
After a miser girlhood, cut the strings
Which tied her money-bags and let them run;
But Emily hoarded — hoarded — only giving
Herself to cold, white paper. Starved and tortured,
She cheated her despair with games of patience
And fooled herself by winning. Frail little elf,
The lonely brain-child of a gaunt maturity,
She hung her womanhood upon a bough
And played ball with the stars — too long — too long —
The garment of herself hung on a tree
Until at last she lost even the desire
To take it down. Whose fault? Why let us say,
To be consistent, Queen Victoria's.
But really, not to over-rate the queen,
I feel obliged to mention Martin Luther,

And behind him the long line of Church Fathers
Who draped their prurience like a dirty cloth
About the naked majesty of God.
Good-bye, my sisters, all of you are great,
And all of you are marvellously strange,
And none of you has any word for me.
. I cannot write like you, I cannot think
In terms of Pagan or of Christian now.
I only hope that possibly some day
Some other woman with an itch for writing
May turn to me as I have turned to you
And chat with me a brief few minutes. How
We lie, we poets! It is three good hours
I have been dreaming. Has it seemed so long
To you? And yet I thank you for the time
Although you leave me sad and self-distrustful,
For older sisters are very sobering things.
Put on your cloaks, my dears, the motor's waiting.
No, you have not seemed strange to me, but near,
Frightfully near, and rather terrifying.
I understand you all, for in myself —
Is that presumption? Yet indeed it's true —
We are one family. And still my answer
Will not be any one of yours, I see.
Well, never mind that now. Good night! Good night!

ON LOOKING AT A COPY OF ALICE MEYNELL'S POEMS, GIVEN ME, YEARS AGO, BY A FRIEND

Upon this greying page you wrote
A whispered greeting, long ago.
Faint pencil-marks run to and fro
Scoring the lines I loved to quote.

A sea-shore of white, shoaling sand,
Blue creeks zigzagging through marsh-grasses,
Sand pipers, and a wind which passes
Cloudily silent up the land.

Upon the high edge of the sea
A great four-master sleeps; three hours
Her bowsprit has not cleared those flowers.
I read and look alternately.

It all comes back again, but dim
As pictures on a winking wall
Hidden save when the dark clouds fall
Or crack to show the moon's bright rim.

I well remember what I was,
And what I wanted. You, unwise

With sore unwisdom, had no eyes
For what was patently the cause.

So are we sport of others' blindness,
We who could see right well alone.
What were you made of — wood or stone?
Yet I remember you with kindness.

You gave this book to me to ease
The smart in me you could not heal.
Your gift a mirror — woe or weal.
We sat beneath the apple-trees.

And I remember how they rang,
These words, like bronze cathedral bells
Down ancient lawns, or citadels
Thundering with gongs where choirs sang.

Silent the sea, the earth, the sky,
And in my heart a silent weeping.
Who has not sown can know no reaping!
Bitter conclusion and no lie.

O heart that sorrows, heart that bleeds,
Heart that was never mine, your words
Were like the pecking Autumn birds
Stealing away my garnered seeds.

No future where there is no past!
O cherishing grief which laid me bare,
I wrapped you like a wintry air
About me. Poor enthusiast!

How strange that tumult, looking back.
The ink is pale, the letters fade.
The verses seem to be well made,
But I have lived the almanac.

And you are dead these drifted years,
How many I forget. And she
Who wrote the book, her tragedy
Long since dried up its scalding tears.

I read of her death yesterday,
Frail lady whom I never knew
And knew so well. Would I could strew
Her grave with pansies, blue and grey.

Would I could stand a little space
Under a blowing, brightening sky,
And watch the sad leaves fall and lie
Gently upon that lonely place.

So cried her heart, a feverish thing.
But clay is still, and clay is cold,
And I was young, and I am old.

And in December what birds sing!

Go, wistful book, go back again
Upon your shelf and gather dust.
I've seen the glitter through the rust
Of old, long years, I've known the pain.

I've recollected both of you,
But I shall recollect no more.
Between us I must shut the door.
The living have so much to do.

GRIEVANCE

ALL these years I have remembered a night
When islands ran black into a sea of silk,
A bay and an open roadstead set to a shimmer like cool,
  white silk
Under an August moon.
Trees lifted themselves softly into the moonlight,
A vine on the balcony glittered with a scattered bril-
  liance,
The roofs of distant houses shone solidly like ice.
Wind passed,
It touched me.
The touch of the wind was cool, impersonal;
The fingers of the wind brushed my face and left me.
I remember that I shivered,
And that the long, continuous sound of the sea beneath
  the cliff
Seemed the endless breathing of the days I must live
  through alone.
I grieve for that night as for something wasted.
You are with me now, but that was twenty years ago,
And the future is shortened by many days.
I no longer fear the length of them,
I dread the swiftness of their departure.

But they go — go —
With the thunderous rapidity of a waterfall,
And scarcely can we find a slow, cool night
To consider ourselves,
And the peaceful shining of the moon
Along a silken sea.

BEHIND TIME

On days when the sky is grey, not blue,
My mind strays back for an age or two,
And amuses itself in a little place
I have made to provide a breathing space
Whenever our twentieth-century air
Heats to a temperature so rare
It stifles fancy, and our thundering cities,
Weighted down by cares and pities,
Load my soul with a heap of dust
Through which no least conceit may thrust
A single stalk or a single bloom
In a free-flung way. Keats made a room
To house him on afternoons like this;
Poe followed him, and created a bliss
Of black and silver furniture;
And Samain, obedient to the lure
Of both these chambers, builded his
Like as a pea, a sort of *bis*
To the others. But Browning broke new ground
In Italy, and what he found
Was "a gash in a wind-grieved Apennine"
With a castle a-top. Now this of mine
Is no rock-perched castle, not even a pink
House of scaling stucco just at the brink

Of a blue Neapolitan bay. Browning's love
Outsoars mine as he soars above
Whatever little there is in me,
I am more modest, as you will see.
My dream is a cottage, trim and neat
As paint can make it, the village street
Runs past, beyond a grove of trees,
But only my gable-ends show through these
To any one walking up and down
The sleepy street of that sea-side town
Where even the fishermen merely fish
When someone's table's in need of a dish
Of oysters, or eels, or cod. My eaves
Peep archly over the bustling leaves
Of Virginia creeper, and down below
The wall-beds glitter with golden glow,
And asters, and black-eyed sun-flowers,
And a strawberry-bush with its dun flowers
That smell of allspice stands at each end
Just where the lawn takes a sudden bend
And turns the corner. A foot or two
From the creaking piazza, a naval review
Of seventy-eights and ninety-fours
Whirls round on a wheel without a pause:
Four-masted schooners luff and jibe,
Fill again with wind, and circumscribe
The limit of their revolution,
And in the centre, the "Constitution"

Points always at the very eye
Of whatever wind is blowing by.
Beyond the lawn, a little cliff
Drops to the shore, held firm and stiff
By rooted broom. The chuckling lap
Of waves on shingle, the sudden flap
Of a fisherman's sail as he hoists it up,
A grumbling rowlock — you may sup
On a sunset silence such as this
Each afternoon. The clematis
Drops a petal on the old sea wall
As purple as the lights which crawl
And melt and flow across the bay,
Whipped green and silver with streaks of grey
Differently mingled every day.
Along the tall horizon slips
A dim procession of sailing ships
So slowly that they scarcely change
Positions from morning till night. The range
Of the telescope planted on the green
Brings illusions of sound where no sound has been,
The bustle of shipboard suddenly grown
Near and clear through the glass half-crown
Of the eye-piece, but take away your eye,
The ships are still as tapestry.
Here is a foot-path, let us go
And see the place where my flowers grow.
Sunken a foot or two below

The bowling-green, my garden lies,
Flanked by hemlocks of every size
Clipped into peacocks and unicorns,
And monstrous dragons for the scorns
Of noble St. Georges. A hedge of thorns
Protects the tiger-lilies set
In rigid rows. The mignonette
Smells sweet, I see a bunch of it
Plucked by a hand which wears a mit,
Just as I see the pansy faces
Peeking from kerchiefs of Mechlin laces,
And note the trace of rowelled spurs
In the monk's-hood bed where a late bee stirs.
Here is a maid and a manikin
Of painted bisque, half-hidden in
An old laburnum's drooping shade.
The little man rests on his spade
And ogles the maiden's broad-brimmed hat
Since he can see nothing of her but that.
Paul and Virginia, he and she,
Mincingly fashioned in pottery.
Now up three steps where the sunlight sifts
Through a thick pleached alley, when one lifts
The latch of the gate, the click as it closes
Is like the snap of buds into roses.
See the little apples are taking shape
And colour above our heads, they gape
And gossip between the latticed leaves.

Look down at your feet where the sunlight
     weaves
Quaint patterns of stems and fruit and we
Walk round in them deliciously.
Now let us go through my open door
And tread the black-and-white-squared floor
And hang our hats on the horns of a deer
I've put in the corner over here.
Four rooms as uneven as carpenter's rule
Ever dared to leave. The first is full
From floor to ceiling of maps and books;
Poetry mostly, by the looks.
Thick little duodecimos,
Slender cloth-covered octavos,
Musty, and fusty, and fingered all,
Make a faded rainbow of each wall.
Within them, faint as a scent of musk
Are words which glimmer through the dusk
Of that vanished world which lies just over
The hither side of each marbled cover.
The fireplace is low and wide
With a rusty crane against the side
And an oven behind, where I keep my cherry
Brandy. Mahogany, pale as sherry,
My writing-table is; the locks
Are brass in the form of crested cocks.
Here are chairs of red and brown
Crumbling leather, pliant as down;

On the arms is manifest
The very spot where my elbows rest
When I balance my mighty folios
And read of men with timber-toes
Who discovered archipelagoes
Or rotted for weeks in a bear-skin tent
With moss for their sole nourishment
Beneath Auroran boreal
Nights for phantasmagorial
Possession of a goodish slice
Of that part of the earth which is nothing but
     ice.
Now cross the hall and I'll introduce
You to something else; a ship's caboose
Saved from the wreck of the Minnie B.
Gone on the sands in seventy-three.
Here is a lantern which used to scan
The foaming wake of an Indiaman;
These chessmen were scrimshawed out of the teeth
Of a whale; that knife in its lacquer sheath
Was filched from the deck of a Chinese junk
A half-an-hour before she sunk
With her pirate crew; this necklace of shells
Was strung for the Indian Jezebels
Of Pitcairn Island, who smiled long years
Ago at the "Bounty" mutineers.
The floor of this room seems to careen
Beneath one's feet, and walls of green

Sea-water to dash against the slim
Matched boards of the sides. I hear the swim
Of a deck-wash sliding from scupper to scupper,
And down through the flanges of the upper
Air, faintly flying above the swell,
The everlasting cry: "All's well!"
Or "There she blows!" or "Breakers ahead!"
I wonder if anything's really dead.
Well, well, there's enough of that. In here
Is a totally different atmosphere.
A pretty shape, this room, the leather
Hangings keep out all notion of weather,
They are Spanish, embossed in gold and blue.
That little picture is a view
Of Venice by Guardi, the Piazzetta
In Carnival, a floweret, a
Shimmer, a perfume, an age in petto
Eighteenth century allegretto.
Considerably unlike it hangs
A Turner, where a mountain's fangs
Close over the plunge of a waterfall
With a slant of sunlight striking it all
To the doom of a planet's evenfall.
Jagged, haggard, splintered steep,
Swept with gold above the deep
Abysmal hollow curving under
The bow of the torrent, grim rotunda
Tawny lit and shocked with thunder.

Here's a picture of nothing but the tops of
      trees,
Wind-blown, cloud overlooked. If you please
'Tis the life-like portrait of a breeze,
No more, no less, what Constable saw
On Hampstead Heath when a brisk cat's-paw
Flurried out of the West-North-West the prize
Of an Autumn morning. I see your eyes
Stray to the corner where stands my spinet.
Suppose we consider it a minute,
Salvator Rosa painted the case
Of satin-wood. Is it out of place
To put a drawing by William Blake
Just above? Does it seem to shake
A symmetry? Perhaps, but it's done.
Observe the rolling, crimson sun
Glitter along the huge outline
Of that weary form, relaxed, supine,
A man on the edge of a rocky world
Balanced above an ocean curled
And frozen. All Eternity
Shouts in that over-borne man for me.
Let us sit awhile and hark to the speech
Of a century beyond our reach,
Colossal, fastidious, witty, brave,
Importuning us from the grave.
Shift on your spindle-legged gold-white chair,
You will not find the answer where

You seek it. Science cannot raise the flap
Between us and these, nor know what gap
Divides Reynolds's, Romney's, Gainsborough's
Population from men like us.
There seems the fragilest sort of partition
Between then and now. By what condition
Do we subscribe to a cruel decree
That what is, for us, is but what we see?
The world shrinks daily; must we confine
Ourselves to a geographer's line,
Choosing our friends by accident
Of almanac? What impertinent
Design is this, which would control
Free intercourse of soul with soul,
Because, forsooth, an airy thing
Brushes us with its bat-like wing,
A thing we cannot see or touch!
Shall such a nothing dare a clutch
At us in passing? So I sit
Considering time and hating it,
Until I glance at that strange clock
Upon the mantel. With a shock,
I see the face is changed, the numbers
Are there no more, something else encumbers
The dial, a half-moon something, writ
About the upper edge of it.
I notice that the iron hands
Point to this crescent, and each stands

Stock still; then I behold the words,
Contrived grotesquely of crossing swords,
And what I read in crimson ink
Is, "It is later than you think!"
I rise and take my latch-key down
And through the peaceful, sleeping town
I walk back to my century,
The dun, dumb years reserved for me
To wander in and call them mine
And be called theirs in every line
Historians may choose to write
Upon my night, my night, my night.

TO A GENTLEMAN WHO WANTED TO SEE THE FIRST DRAFTS OF MY POEMS IN THE INTERESTS OF PSY-CHOLOGICAL RESEARCH INTO THE WORKINGS OF THE CREATIVE MIND

So you want to see my papers, look what I have written
    down
'Twixt an ecstasy and heartbreak, con them over with a
    frown.
You would watch my thought's green sprouting ere a
    single blossom's blown.

Would you, friend? And what should I be doing, have
    you thought of that?
Is it pleasant, think you, being gazed upon from feet to
    hat,
Microscopically viewed by eyes commissioned just for
    that?

Don't assure me that your interest does not lie with me
    at all.
I'm a poet to be dissected for the good of science. Call
It by any name, I feel like some old root where fungi
    sprawl.

Think you, I could make you see it, all the little diverse
    strands
Locked in one short poem? By no means do I find your
    prying hands
Pleasure bearing and delightful straying round my lotus
    lands.

Not a word but joins itself with some adventure I alone
Could attach consideration to. You'd wrench me flesh
    from bone,
Find the heart and count its tappings. At your touch,
    'twould turn to stone.

What is I, and what that other? That's your quest.
    I'll have you know
Telling it would break it from me, it would melt like
    travelled snow.
I will be no weary pathway for another's feet to go.

Seize the butterfly and wing it, thus you learn of butter-
    flies.
But you do not ask permission of the creature, which is
    wise.
If I did consent, to please you, I should tell you packs of
    lies.

To one only will I tell it, do I tell it all day long.

Only one can see the patches I work into quilts of
    song.
Crazy quilts, I'm sure you'd deem them, quite unworthy
    of your prong.

One must go half-way with poets, feel the thing you're
    out to find,
Wonder even while you name it, keep it somehow still
    enshrined,
Still encased within its leafage like an arbour honey-
    vined.

Lacking just this touch and tremour, how can I but
    shrink and clutch
What I have to closer keeping. Little limping phan-
    toms, such
Are my poems before I've taught them how to walk
    without a crutch.

You mean well, I do not doubt it, but you're blind as
    any mule.
Would you question a mad lover, set his love-making to
    rule?
With your pulse upon his finger, watch him play the
    sighing fool?

Would he win the lady, tell me, with you by? Your
    calculations

Might frustrate a future teeming with immeasurable
    equations.
Which will prove the most important, your research or
    his relations?

Take my answer then, for, flatly, I will not be vivisected.
Life is more to me than learning. If you clumsily de-
    flected
My contact with what I know not, could it surely be
    connected?

Scarcely could you, knowing nothing, swear to me it
    would be so.
Therefore unequivocally, brazenly, I tell you, "No!"
To the fame of an avowal, I prefer my domino.

Still I have a word, one moment, stop, before you leave
    this room.
Though I shudder thinking of you wandring through my
    beds of bloom,
You may come with spade and shovel when I'm safely
    in the tomb.

THE SLIPPERS OF THE GODDESS
OF BEAUTY

" It is easy, like Momus, to find fault with the clattering of the slipper worn by the Goddess of beauty ; but ' the serious Gods ' found better employment in admiration of her unapproachable loveliness."

THEY clatter, clatter, clatter on the floor,
Her slippers clack upon the marble slabs,
And every time her heels clap, I count one,
And go on counting till my nerves are sick
With one and one and one told out in claps.

He shot a hand out, clutching at my arm
With bony fingers. "Young man," said he, "look up.
Is that a starry face, or am I blind?
Do stars beset her like a crown of pearls?
Does sunset tinge and tangle in her hair,
And moonlight rush in silver from her breasts?
Look well, young man, for maybe I am blind."
I looked, and agony assailed my brain.
He chirruped at me. "So — so! Ancient eyes
Know better than to keep upon the floor.
What dazzles you is kindly sight to me,
One gets accustomed. But I interrupt

Your count. What figure had you reached?" I shook
Him off and staggered to my room, bright pain
Stabbing my head.

                I've never found that count,
Nor started on another. Every day
I look a little longer when she comes,
And see a little more, and bear to see.
But that queer man I've never met again,
Nor very much desired to, perhaps.
Gratitude is an irksome thing to youth,
And I, thank Hermes, am still reckoned young,
Though old enough to look above the floor,
Which is a certain age, I must admit.
But I'll endure that, seeing what it brings.

THE CAPTURED GODDESS

OVER the housetops,
Above the rotating chimney-pots,
I have seen a shiver of amethyst,
And blue and cinnamon have flickered
A moment,
At the far end of a dusty street.

Through sheeted rain
Has come a lustre of crimson,
And I have watched moonbeams
Hushed by a film of palest green.

It was her wings,
Goddess!
Who stepped over the clouds,
And laid her rainbow feathers
Aslant on the currents of the air.

I followed her for long,
With gazing eyes and stumbling feet.
I cared not where she led me,
My eyes were full of colours:

Saffrons, rubies, the yellows of beryls,
And the indigo-blue of quartz;
Flights of rose, layers of chrysoprase,
Points of orange, spirals of vermilion,
The spotted gold of tiger-lily petals,
The loud pink of bursting hydrangeas.
I followed,
And watched for the flashing of her wings.

In the city I found her,
The narrow-streeted city.
In the market-place I came upon her,
Bound and trembling.
Her fluted wings were fastened to her sides with cords,
She was naked and cold,
For that day the wind blew
Without sunshine.

Men chaffered for her,
They bargained in silver and gold,
In copper, in wheat,
And called their bids across the market-place.

The Goddess wept.

Hiding my face I fled,
And the grey wind hissed behind me,
Along the narrow streets.

ASTIGMATISM

To Ezra Pound

WITH MUCH FRIENDSHIP AND ADMIRATION AND
SOME DIFFERENCES OF OPINION

The Poet took his walking-stick
Of fine and polished ebony.
Set in the close-grained wood
Were quaint devices;
Patterns in ambers,
And in the clouded green of jades.
The top was of smooth, yellow ivory,
And a tassel of tarnished gold
Hung by a faded cord from a hole
Pierced in the hard wood,
Circled with silver.
For years the Poet had wrought upon this cane.
His wealth had gone to enrich it,
His experiences to pattern it,
His labour to fashion and burnish it.
To him it was perfect,
A work of art and a weapon,
A delight and a defence.
The Poet took his walking-stick
And walked abroad.

Peace be with you, Brother.

The Poet came to a meadow.
Sifted through the grass were daisies,
Open-mouthed, wondering, they gazed at the sun.
The Poet struck them with his cane.
The little heads flew off, and they lay
Dying, open-mouthed and wondering,
On the hard ground.
"They are useless. They are not roses," said the Poet.

Peace be with you, Brother. Go your ways.

The Poet came to a stream.
Purple and blue flags waded in the water;
In among them hopped the speckled frogs;
The wind slid through them, rustling.
The Poet lifted his cane,
And the iris heads fell into the water.
They floated away, torn and drowning.
"Wretched flowers," said the Poet,
"They are not roses."

Peace be with you, Brother. It is your affair.

The Poet came to a garden.

Dahlias ripened against a wall,
Gillyflowers stood up bravely for all their short stature,
And a trumpet-vine covered an arbour
With the red and gold of its blossoms.
Red and gold like the brass notes of trumpets.
The Poet knocked off the stiff heads of the dahlias,
And his cane lopped the gillyflowers at the ground.
Then he severed the trumpet-blossoms from their stems.
Red and gold they lay scattered,
Red and gold, as on a battle field;
Red and gold, prone and dying.
"They were not roses," said the Poet.

Peace be with you, Brother.
But behind you is destruction, and waste places.

The Poet came home at evening,
And in the candle-light
He wiped and polished his cane.
The orange candle flame leaped in the yellow ambers,
And made the jades undulate like green pools.
It played along the bright ebony,
And glowed in the top of cream-coloured ivory.
But these things were dead,
Only the candle-light made them seem to move.
"It is a pity there were no roses," said the Poet.

Peace be with you, Brother. You have chosen your part.

TO CARL SANDBURG

I THINK I am cousin-german to Endymion,
Certainly I have loved the moon a long time.

I have seen her, a faint conceit of silver,
Shooting little silver arrows into a marsh pool at twi-
    light.
I have seen her, high, round, majestic,
Making herself a jewel of fire out of a sea bay.
I have seen the morning moon, grievously battered,
Limping down a coloured sky.
To-night I saw an evening moon
Dodging between tree-branches
Through a singing silence of crickets,
And a man was singing songs to a black-backed guitar.

To-day I saw a country I knew well but had never seen.
A country where corn runs a mile or more to a tree-line,
A country where a river, brown as bronze, streaked
    green with the flowing heads of water-plants,
Slips between a field of apples and a field of wheat.
A country where the eye seeks a long way
And comes back on the curve of a round sky,

Satisfied with greens and blues, tired with the stretch
    and exhilarated by it.

The moon stops a moment in a hole between leaves
And tells me a new story,
The story of a man who lives in a house with a pear-tree
    before the door,
A story of little green pears changing and ripening,
Of long catalpa pods turning yellow through September
    days.
There is a woman in the house, and children,
And, out beyond, the corn-fields are sleeping and the
    trees are whispering to the fire-flies.
So I have seen the man's country, and heard his songs
    before there are words to them.
And the moon said to me: "This now I give you," and
    went on, stepping through the leaves.
And the man went on singing, picking out his accom-
    paniment softly on the black-backed guitar.

ELEONORA DUSE

I

Seeing's believing, so the ancient word
Chills buds to shrivelled powder flecks, turns flax
To smoky heaps of straw whose small flames wax
Only to gasp and die. The thing's absurd!
Have blind men ever seen or deaf men heard?
What one beholds but measures what one lacks.
Where is the prism to draw gold from blacks,
Or flash the iris colours of a bird?
Not in the eye, be sure, nor in the ear,
Nor in an instrument of twisted glass,
Yet there are sights I see and sounds I hear
Which ripple me like water as they pass.
This that I give you for a dear love's sake
Is curling noise of waves marching along a lake.

II

A letter or a poem — the words are set
To either tune.   Be careful how you slice
The flap which is held down by this device
Impressed upon it.   In one moment met
A cameo, intaglio, a fret

Of workmanship, and I. Like melted ice
I took the form and froze so, turned precise
And brittle seal, a creed in silhouette.
Seeing's believing? What then would you see?
A chamfered dragon? Three spear-heads of
    steel?
A motto done in flowered charactry?
The thin outline of Mercury's winged heel?
Look closer, do you see a name, a face,
Or just a cloud dropped down before a holy
    place?

III

Lady, to whose enchantment I took shape
So long ago, though carven to your grace,
Bearing, like quickened wood, your sweet sad
    face
Cut in my flesh, yet may I not escape
My limitations: words that jibe and gape
After your loveliness and make grimace
And travesty where they should interlace
The weave of sun-spun ocean round a cape.
Pictures then must contain you, this and more,
The sigh of wind floating on ripe June hay,
The desolate pulse of snow beyond a door,
The grief of mornings seen as yesterday.
All that you are mingles as one sole cry
To point a world aright which is so much awry.

IV

If Beauty set her image on a stage
And bid it mirror moments so intense
With passion and swift largess of the sense
To a divine exactness, stamp a page
With mottoes of hot blood, and disengage
No atom of mankind's experience,
But lay the soul's complete incontinence
Bare while it tills grief's gusty acreage.
Doing this, you, spon-image to her needs,
She picked to pierce, reveal, and soothe again,
Shattering by means of you the tinsel creeds
Offered as meat to the pinched hearts of men.
So, sacrificing you, she fed those others
Who bless you in their prayers even before
            their mothers.

V

Life seized you with her iron hands and shook
The fire of your boundless burning out
To fall on us, poor little ragged rout
Of common men, till like a flaming book
We, letters of a message, flashed and took
The fiery flare of prophecy, devout
Torches to bear your oil, a dazzling shout,
The liquid golden running of a brook.
Who, being upborne on racing streams of light,

Seeing new heavens sprung from dusty hells,
Considered you, and what might be your plight,
Robbed, plundered — since Life's cruel plan compels
The perfect sacrifice of one great soul
To make a myriad others even a whit more whole.

VI

Seeing you stand once more before my eyes
In your pale dignity and tenderness,
Wearing your frailty like a misty dress
Draped over the great glamour which denies
To years their domination, all disguise
Time can achieve is but to add a stress,
A finer fineness, as though some caress
Touched you a moment to a strange surprise.
Seeing you after these long lengths of years,
I only know the glory come again,
A majesty bewildered by my tears,
A golden sun spangling slant shafts of rain,
Moonlight delaying by a sick man's bed,
A rush of daffodils where wastes of dried leaves
      spread.

TO JOHN KEATS

GREAT master! Boyish, sympathetic man!
  Whose orbed and ripened genius lightly hung
  From life's slim, twisted tendril and there swung
In crimson-sphered completeness; guardian
Of crystal portals through whose openings fan
  The spicéd winds which blew when earth was young,
  Scattering wreaths of stars, as Jove once flung
A golden shower from heights cerulean.
  Crumbled before thy majesty we bow.
  Forget thy empurpled state, thy panoply
Of greatness, and be merciful and near;
  A youth who trudged the highroad we tread now
  Singing the miles behind him; so may we
Faint throbbings of thy music overhear.

ON READING A LINE UNDERSCORED BY KEATS

IN A COPY OF "PALMERIN OF ENGLAND"

You marked it with light pencil upon a printed page,
And, as though your finger pointed along a sunny path
     for my eyes' better direction,
I see "a knight mounted on a mulberry courser and at-
     tired in green armour."
I think the sky is faintly blue, but with a Spring shining
     about it,
And the new grass scarcely fetlock high in the meads.
He rides, I believe, alongside an overflown river,
By a path soft and easy to his charger's feet.
My vision confuses you with the green-armoured
     knight:
So dight and caparisoned might you be in a land of
     Faery.
Thus, with denoting finger, you make of yourself an
     escutcheon to guide me to that in you which is
     its essence.
But for the rest,
The part which most persists and is remembered,
I only know I compass it in loving and neither have, nor
     need, a symbol.

THE ENCHANTED CASTLE
To Edgar Allan Poe

Old crumbling stones set long ago upon
The naked headland of a suave green shore.
Old stones all riven into cracks and glands
By moss and ivy. Up above, a peak
Of narrow, iron windows, a hooded tower
With frozen windows looking to the West.
When the sun sets, a winking, fiery light
Riffles the window-panes above the gloom
Of purple waters heaving evenly,
Waters moving about the naked headland
In sombre slowness, with no dash of spray
To strike the stagnant pools and flash the weeds.
                              A rack of shifting clouds
Darkens the waters' margin. On the shore
Are clusters of great trees whose brittle leaves
Crackle together as the mournful wind
Takes them and shakes them. But the tower windows
Fling bloody streams of light across the dusk,
Planges of bloody light which the upper sky
Has hurled at them and now is drawing back.
Behind the tower, where no windows are,
A little wisp of moon catches the stones
So that they glitter palely from the shore,
The suave green shore with all its leaden trees.

A BATHER

After a Picture by Andreas Zorn

THICK dappled by circles of sunshine and fluttering
    shade,
Your bright, naked body advances, blown over by
    leaves,
Half-quenched in their various green, just a point of you
    showing,
A knee or a thigh, sudden glimpsed, then at once blotted
    into
The filmy and flickering forest, to start out again
Triumphant in smooth, supple roundness, edged sharp
    as white ivory,
Cool, perfect, with rose rarely tinting your lips and your
    breasts,
Swelling out from the green in the opulent curves of ripe
    fruit,
And hidden, like fruit, by the swift intermittence of
    leaves.
So, clinging to branches and moss, you advance on the
    ledges
Of rock which hang over the stream, with the wood-
    smells about you,
The pungence of strawberry plants, and of gum-
    oozing spruces,

While below runs the water, impatient, impatient — to
    take you,
To splash you, to run down your sides, to sing you of
    deepness,
Of pools brown and golden, with brown-and-gold flags
    on their borders,
Of blue, lingering skies floating solemnly over your
    beauty,
Of undulant waters a-sway in the effort to hold you,
To keep you submerged and quiescent while over you
    glories
The Summer.

                Oread, Dryad, or Naiad, or just
Woman, clad only in youth and in gallant perfection,
Standing up in a great burst of sunshine, you dazzle my
    eyes
Like a snow-star, a moon, your effulgence burns up in a
    halo,
For you are the chalice which holds all the races of men.

You slip into the pool and the water folds over your
    shoulder,
And over the tree-tops the clouds slowly follow your
    swimming,
And the scent of the woods is sweet on this hot Summer
    morning.

VIOLIN SONATA BY VINCENT D'INDY

To Charles Martin Loeffler

A LITTLE brown room in a sea of fields,
Fields pink as rose-mallows
Under a fading rose-mallow sky.

Four candles on a tall iron candlestick,
Clustered like altar lights.
Above, the models of four brown Chinese junks
Sailing round the brown walls,
Silent and motionless.

The quick cut of a vibrating string,
Another, and another,
Biting into the silence.
Notes pierce, sharper and sharper;
They draw up in a freshness of sound,
Higher — higher, to the whiteness of intolerable beauty.
They are jagged and clear,
Like snow peaks against the sky;
They hurt like air too pure to breathe.
Is it catgut and horsehair,
Or flesh sawing against the cold blue gates of the sky?

The brown Chinese junks sail silently round the brown
      walls.

A cricket hurries across the bare floor.

The windows are black, for the sun has set.

Only the candles,
Clustered like altar lamps upon their tall candlestick,
Light the violinist as he plays.

CHOPIN

THE cat and I
Together in the sultry night
Waited.
He greatly desired a mouse;
I, an idea.
Neither ambition was gratified.
So we watched
In a stiff and painful expectation.
Little breezes pattered among the trees,
And thin stars ticked at us
Faintly,
Exhausted pulses
Squeezing through mist.

Those others, I said!
And my mind rang hollow as I tapped it.
Winky, I said,
Do all other cats catch their mice?

      *   *   *   *   *   *

It was low and long,
Ivory white, with doors and windows blotting
        blue upon it.

Wind choked in pomegranate-trees,
Rain rattled on lead roofs,
And stuttered along twisted conduit-pipes.
An eagle screamed out of the heavy sky,
And some one in the house screamed
"Ah, I knew that you were dead!"

So that was it:
Funeral chants,
And the icy cowls of buried monks;
Organs on iron midnights,
And long wax winding-sheets
Guttered from altar candles.

First this,
Then spitting blood.
Music quenched in blood,
Flights of arpeggios confused by blood,
Flute-showers of notes stung and arrested on a sharp
        chord,
Tangled in a web of blood.
" I cannot send you the manuscripts, as they are not yet
        finished.
I have been ill as a dog.
My illness has had a pernicious effect on the Preludes
Which you will receive God knows when."

        *   *   *   *   *   *

He bore it.

Therefore, Winky, drink some milk
And leave the mouse until to-morrow.
There are no blood-coloured pomegranate flowers
Hurling their petals in at the open window,
But you can sit in my lap
And blink at a bunch of cinnamon-eyed coreopsis
While I pull your ears
In the manner which you find so infinitely agreeable.

MUSIC

THE neighbour sits in his window and plays the flute.
From my bed I can hear him,
And the round notes flutter and tap about the room,
And hit against each other,
Blurring to unexpected chords.
It is very beautiful,
With the little flute-notes all about me,
In the darkness.

In the daytime,
The neighbour eats bread and onions with one hand
And copies music with the other.
He is fat and has a bald head,
So I do not look at him,
But run quickly past his window.
There is always the sky to look at,
Or the water in the well!

But when night comes and he plays his flute,
I think of him as a young man,
With gold seals hanging from his watch,
And a blue coat with silver buttons.
As I lie in my bed
The flute-notes push against my ears and lips,
And I go to sleep, dreaming.

THE CONGRESSIONAL LIBRARY

THE earth is a coloured thing.
See the red clays, and the umbers and salt greys of the
    mountains;
See the clustered and wandering greens of plains and
    hillsides,
The leaf-greens, bush-greens, water-plant and snow-
    greens
Of gardens and forests.
See the reds of flowers — hibiscus, poppy, geranium;
The rose-red of little flowers — may-flowers, primroses;
The harlequin shades of sweet-peas, orchids, pansies;
The madders, saffrons, chromes, of still waters,
The silver and star-blues, the wine-blues of seas and
    oceans.
Observe the stars at night time, name the colour of
    them;
Count and recount the hues of clouds at sunset and at
    dawn.
And the colours of the races of men —
What are they?
And what are we?
We, the people without a race,
Without a language;
Of all races, and of none;

Of all tongues, and one imposed;
Of all traditions and all pasts,
With no tradition and no past.
A patchwork and an altar-piece,
Vague as sea-mist,
Myriad as forest-trees,
Living into a present,
Building a future.
Our colour is the vari-coloured world.
No colours clash,
All clash and change,
And, in changing, new colours come and go and
        dominate and remain,
And no one shall say which remain,
Since those that have vanished return,
And those no man has seen take the light and are.

Where else in all America are we so symbolized
As in this hall?
White columns polished like glass,
A dome and a dome,
A balcony and a balcony,
Stairs and the balustrades to them,
Yellow marble and red slabs of it,
All mounting, spearing, flying into colour.
Colour round the dome and up to it,
Colour curving, kite-flying, to the second dome,
Light, dropping, pitching down upon the colour,

Arrow-falling upon the glass-bright pillars,
Mingled colours spinning into a shape of white pillars,
Fusing, cooling, into balanced shafts of shrill and inter-
       thronging light.
This is America,
This vast, confused beauty,
This staring, restless speed of loveliness,
Mighty, overwhelming, crude, of all forms,
Making grandeur out of profusion,
Afraid of no incongruities,
Sublime in its audacity,
Bizarre breaker of moulds,
Laughing with strength,
Charging down on the past,
Glorious and conquering,
Destroyer, builder,
Invincible pith and marrow of the world,
An old world remaking,
Whirling into the no-world of all-coloured light.

But behind the vari-coloured hall?
The entrails, the belly,
The blood-run veins, the heart and viscera,
What of these?
Only at night do they speak,
Only at night do the voices rouse themselves and speak.
There are words in the veins of this creature,
There are still notes singing in its breast:

Silent voices, whispering what it shall speak,
Frozen music beating upon its pulses.
These are the voices of the furious dead who never die,
Furious with love and life, unquenchable,
Dictating their creeds across the vapours of time.
This is the music of the Trumpeters of the Almighty
Weeping for a lost estate,
Sounding to a new birth which is to-morrow.
Hark! This hurricane of music has no end,
The speech of these voices has neither end nor beginning;
They are inter-riven as the colours of the sky
Over the graveyards of ten thousand generations.

When we are as Nineveh, our white columns thrown and
        scattered,
Our dome of colours striped with the crawling of insects,
Spotted with the thrust of damp clay —
Our words, our music, who will build a dome to hive
        them?
In whose belly shall we come to life?
A new life,
Beyond submergence and destruction,
The implacable life of silent words,
Of tumultuous stillness of never-ceasing music,
Lost to being that so it may triumph
And become the blood and heat and urge
Of that hidden distance which forever whips and harries
        the static present
Of mankind.

AN AQUARIUM

STREAKS of green and yellow iridescence,
Silver shiftings,
Rings veering out of rings,
Silver — gold —
Grey-green opaqueness sliding down,
With sharp white bubbles
Shooting and dancing,
Flinging quickly outward.
Nosing the bubbles,
Swallowing them,
Fish.
Blue shadows against silver-saffron water,
The light rippling over them
In steel-bright tremors.
Outspread translucent fins
Flute, fold, and relapse;
The threaded light prints through them on the pebbles
In scarcely tarnished twinklings.
Curving of spotted spines,
Slow up-shifts,
Lazy convolutions:
Then a sudden swift straightening
And darting below:

Oblique grey shadows
Athwart a pale casement.
Roped and curled,
Green man-eating eels
Slumber in undulate rhythms,
With crests laid horizontal on their backs.
Barred fish,
Striped fish,
Uneven disks of fish,
Slip, slide, whirl, turn,
And never touch.
Metallic blue fish,
With fins wide and yellow and swaying
Like Oriental fans,
Hold the sun in their bellies
And glow with light:
Blue brilliance cut by black bars.
An oblong pane of straw-coloured shimmer,
Across it, in a tangent,
A smear of rose, black, silver.
Short twists and upstartings,
Rose-black, in a setting of bubbles:
Sunshine playing between red and black flowers
On a blue and gold lawn.
Shadows and polished surfaces,
Facets of mauve and purple,
A constant modulation of values.
Shaft-shaped,

With green bead eyes;
Thick-nosed,
Heliotrope-coloured;
Swift spots of chrysolite and coral;
In the midst of green, pearl, amethyst irradiations.

Outside,
A willow-tree flickers
With little white jerks,
And long blue waves
Rise steadily beyond the outer islands.

THE PIKE

In the brown water,
Thick and silver-sheened in the sunshine,
Liquid and cool in the shade of the reeds,
A pike dozed.
Lost among the shadows of stems
He lay unnoticed.
Suddenly he flicked his tail,
And a green-and-copper brightness
Ran under the water.

Out from under the reeds
Came the olive-green light,
And orange flashed up
Through the sun-thickened water.
So the fish passed across the pool,
Green and copper,
A darkness and a gleam,
And the blurred reflections of the willows on
        the opposite bank
Received it.

CONVALESCENCE

FROM out the dragging vastness of the sea,
  Wave-fettered, bound in sinuous, seaweed strands,
  He toils toward the rounding beach, and stands
One moment, white and dripping, silently,
Cut like a cameo in lazuli,
  Then falls, betrayed by shifting shells, and lands
  Prone in the jeering water, and his hands
Clutch for support where no support can be.
  So up, and down, and forward, inch by inch,
He gains upon the shore, where poppies glow
And sandflies dance their little lives away.
  The sucking waves retard, and tighter clinch
The weeds about him, but the land-winds blow,
And in the sky there blooms the sun of May.

NIGHTMARE: A TALE FOR AN AUTUMN EVENING

After a Print by George Cruikshank

It was a gusty night,
With the wind booming, and swooping,
Looping round corners,
Sliding over the cobble-stones,
Whipping and veering,
And careering over the roofs
Like a thousand clattering horses.
Mr. Spruggins had been dining in the city,
Mr. Spruggins was none too steady in his gait,
And the wind played ball with Mr. Spruggins
And laughed as it whistled past him.
It rolled him along the street,
With his little feet pit-a-patting on the flags of the side-
        walk,
And his muffler and his coat-tails blown straight out be-
        hind him.
It bumped him against area railings,
And chuckled in his ear when he said "Ouch!"
Sometimes it lifted him clear off his little patting feet
And bore him in triumph over three grey flagstones and
        a quarter.

The moon dodged in and out of clouds, winking.

It was all very unpleasant for Mr. Spruggins,

And when the wind flung him hard against his own
      front door

It was a relief,

Although the breath was quite knocked out of him.

The gas-lamp in front of the house flared up,

And the keyhole was as big as a barn door;

The gas-lamp flickered away to a sputtering blue star,

And the keyhole went out with it.

Such a stabbing, and jabbing,

And sticking, and picking,

And poking, and pushing, and prying

With that key;

And there is no denying that Mr. Spruggins rapped out
      an oath or two,

Rub-a-dub-dubbing them out to a real snare-drum roll.

But the door opened at last,

And Mr. Spruggins blew through it into his own hall

And slammed the door to so hard

That the knocker banged five times before it stopped.

Mr. Spruggins struck a light and lit a candle,

And all the time the moon winked at him through the
      window.

"Why couldn't you find the keyhole, Spruggins?"

Taunted the wind.

"I can find the keyhole."

And the wind, thin as a wire,

Darted in and seized the candle flame
And knocked it over to one side
And pummelled it down — down — down —!
But Mr. Spruggins held the candle so close that it singed
his chin,
And ran and stumbled up the stairs in a surprisingly
agile manner,
For the wind through the keyhole kept saying, "Sprug-
gins! Spruggins!" behind him.
The fire in his bedroom burned brightly.
The room with its crimson bed and window curtains
Was as red and glowing as a carbuncle.
It was still and warm.
There was no wind here, for the windows were fastened;
And no moon,
For the curtains were drawn.
The candle flame stood up like a pointed pear
In a wide brass dish.
Mr. Spruggins sighed with content;
He was safe at home.
The fire glowed — red and yellow roses
In the black basket of the grate —
And the bed with its crimson hangings
Seemed a great peony,
Wide open and placid.
Mr. Spruggins slipped off his top-coat and his muffler.
He slipped off his bottle-green coat
And his flowered waistcoat.

He put on a flannel dressing-gown,
And tied a peaked night-cap under his chin.
He wound his large gold watch
And placed it under his pillow.
Then he tiptoed over to the window and pulled back the
          curtain.
There was the moon dodging in and out of the clouds;
But behind him was his quiet candle.
There was the wind whisking along the street.
The window rattled, but it was fastened.
Did the wind say, "Spruggins"?
All Mr. Spruggins heard was "S-s-s-s-s —"
Dying away down the street.
He dropped the curtain and got into bed.
Martha had been in the last thing with the warming-
          pan;
The bed was warm,
And Mr. Spruggins sank into feathers,
With the familiar ticking of his watch just under his
          head.
Mr. Spruggins dozed.
He had forgotten to put out the candle,
But it did not make much difference as the fire was so
          bright . . .
Too bright!
The red and yellow roses pricked his eyelids,
They scorched him back to consciousness.
He tried to shift his position;

He could not move.

Something weighed him down,

He could not breathe.

He was gasping,

Pinned down and suffocating.

He opened his eyes.

The curtains of the window were flung back,

The fire and the candle were out,

And the room was filled with green moonlight.

And pressed against the window-pane

Was a wide, round face,

Winking — winking —

Solemnly dropping one eyelid after the other.

Tick — tock — went the watch under his pillow,

Wink — wink — went the face at the window.

It was not the fire roses which had pricked him,

It was the winking eyes.

Mr. Spruggins tried to bounce up;

He could not, because —

His heart flapped up into his mouth

And fell back dead.

On his chest was a fat pink pig,

On the pig a blackamoor

With a ten pound weight for a cap.

His mustachios kept curling up and down like angry
        snakes,

And his eyes rolled round and round,

With the pupils coming into sight, and disappearing,

And appearing again on the other side.

The holsters at his saddle-bow were two port bottles,

And a curved table-knife hung at his belt for a scimitar,

While a fork and a keg of spirits were strapped to the
      saddle behind.

He dug his spurs into the pig,

Which trampled and snorted,

And stamped its cloven feet deeper into Mr. Spruggins.

Then the green light on the floor began to undulate.

It heaved and hollowed,

It rose like a tide,

Sea-green,

Full of claws and scales

And wriggles.

The air above his bed began to move;

It weighed over him

In a mass of draggled feathers.

Not one lifted to stir the air.

They drooped and dripped

With a smell of port wine and brandy,

Closing down, slowly,

Trickling drops on the bed-quilt.

Suddenly the window fell in with a great scatter of glass,

And the moon burst into the room,

Sizzling —"S-s-s-s — Spruggins! Spruggins!"

It rolled toward him,

A green ball of flame,

With two eyes in the center,

A red eye and a yellow eye,
Dropping their lids slowly,
One after the other.
Mr. Spruggins tried to scream,
But the blackamoor
Leapt off his pig
With a cry,
Drew his scimitar,
And plunged it into Mr. Spruggins's mouth.

Mr. Spruggins got up in the cold dawn
And remade the fire.
Then he crept back to bed
By the light which seeped in under the window curtains,
And lay there, shivering,
While the bells of St. George the Martyr chimed the
          quarter after seven.

EVELYN RAY

No decent man will cross a field
Laid down to hay, until its yield

Is cut and cocked, yet there was the track
Going in from the lane and none coming back.

But that was afterwards; before,
The field was smooth as a sea off shore

On a shimmering afternoon, waist-high
With bent, and red top, and timothy,

Lush with oat grass and tall fescue,
And the purple green of Kentucky blue;

A noble meadow, so broad each way
It took three good scythes to mow in a day.

Just where the field broke into a wood
A knotted old catalpa stood,

And in the old catalpa-tree
A cat-bird sang immoderately.

The sky above him was round and big
And its centre seemed just over his twig.

The earth below him was fresh and fair,
With the sun's long fingers everywhere.

The cat-bird perched where a great leaf hung,
And the great leaf tilted, and flickered, and
      swung.

The cat-bird sang with a piercing glee
Up in the sun-specked catalpa-tree.

He sang so loud and he sang so long
That his ears were drowned in his own sweet song.

But the little peering leaves of grass
Shook and sundered to let them pass,

To let them pass, the men who heard
Nothing the grass said, nothing the bird.

Each man was still as a shining stone,
Each man's head was a buzzing bone

Wherein two words screeched in and out
Like a grinding saw with its turn about:

"Evelyn Ray," each stone man said,
And the words cut back and forth through his head
And each of them wondered if he were dead.

The cat-bird sang with his head cocked up
Gazing into the sky's blue cup.

The grasses waved back into place,
The sun's long fingers stroked each face,

Each grim, cold face that saw no sun.
And the feet led the faces on and on.

They stopped beside the catalpa-tree,
Said one stone face to the other: "See!"

The other face had nothing to say,
Its lips were frozen on "Evelyn Ray."

They laid their hats in the tall green grass
Where the crickets and grasshoppers pass and pass.

They hung their coats in the crotch of a pine
And paced five feet in an even line.

They measured five paces either way,
And the saws in their heads screeched "Evelyn Ray."

The cat-bird sang so loud and clear
He heard nothing at all, there was nothing to hear.

Even the swish of long legs pushing
Through grass had ceased, there was only the hush-
                    ing

Of a windless wind in the daisy tops,
And the jar stalks make when a grasshopper hops.

Every now and then a bee boomed over
The black-eyed Susans in search of clover,

And crickets shrilled as crickets do:
One — two. One — two.

The cat-bird sang with his head in the air,
And the sun's bright fingers poked here and there,

Past leaf, and branch, and needle, and cone.
But the stone men stood like men of stone.

Each man lifted a dull stone hand
And his fingers felt like weaving sand,

And his feet seemed standing on a ball
Which tossed and turned in a waterfall.

Each man heard a shot somewhere
Dropping out of the distant air.

But the screaming saws no longer said
"Evelyn Ray," for the men were dead.

    *   *   *   *   *   *

I often think of Evelyn Ray.
What did she do, what did she say?
Did she ever chance to pass that way?

I remember it as a lovely spot
Where a cat-bird sang. When he heard the shot,
Did he fly away? I have quite forgot.

When I went there last, he was singing again
Through a little fleeting, misty rain,
And pine-cones lay where they had lain.

This is the tale as I heard it when
I was young from a man who was threescore
      and ten.
A lady of clay and two stone men.

A pretty problem is here, no doubt,
If you have a fancy to work it out:
What happens to stone when clay is about?

Muse upon it as long as you will,
I think myself it will baffle your skill,
And your answer will be what mine is — nil.

But every sunny Summer's day
I am teased with the thought of Evelyn Ray,
Poor little image of painted clay.
And Heigh-o! I say.
What if there be a judgment-day?

What if all religions be true,
And Gabriel's trumpet blow for you
And blow for them — what will you do?

Evelyn Ray, will you rise alone?
Or will your lovers of dull grey stone
Pace beside you through the wan

Twilight of that bitter day
To be judged as stone and judged as clay,
And no one to say the judgment nay?

Better be nothing, Evelyn Ray,
A handful of buttercups that sway
In the wind for a children's holiday.

For earth to earth is the best we know,
Where the good blind worms push to and fro

Turning us into the seeds which grow,

And lovers and ladies are dead indeed,
Lost in the sap of a flower seed.
Is this, think you, a sorry creed?

Well, be it so, for the world is wide
And opinions jostle on every side.
What has always hidden will always hide.

And every year when the fields are high
With oat grass, and red top, and timothy,
I know that a creed is the shell of a lie.

Peace be with you, Evelyn Ray,
And to your lovers, if so it may,
For earth made stone and earth made clay.

PATTERNS

I WALK down the garden paths,
And all the daffodils
Are blowing, and the bright blue squills.
I walk down the patterned garden-paths
In my stiff, brocaded gown.
With my powdered hair and jewelled fan,
I too am a rare
Pattern. As I wander down
The garden paths.

My dress is richly figured,
And the train
Makes a pink and silver stain
On the gravel, and the thrift
Of the borders.
Just a plate of current fashion,
Tripping by in high-heeled, ribboned shoes.
Not a softness anywhere about me,
Only whalebone and brocade.
And I sink on a seat in the shade
Of a lime tree. For my passion
Wars against the stiff brocade.
The daffodils and squills

Flutter in the breeze
As they please.
And I weep;
For the lime-tree is in blossom
And one small flower has dropped upon my bosom.

And the plashing of waterdrops
In the marble fountain
Comes down the garden-paths.
The dripping never stops.
Underneath my stiffened gown
Is the softness of a woman bathing in a marble basin,
A basin in the midst of hedges grown
So thick, she cannot see her lover hiding,
But she guesses he is near,
And the sliding of the water
Seems the stroking of a dear
Hand upon her.
What is Summer in a fine brocaded gown!
I should like to see it lying in a heap upon the ground.
All the pink and silver crumpled up on the ground.

I would be the pink and silver as I ran along the paths,
And he would stumble after,
Bewildered by my laughter.
I should see the sun flashing from his sword-hilt and the
        buckles on his shoes.
I would choose

To lead him in a maze along the patterned paths,
A bright and laughing maze for my heavy-booted lover.
Till he caught me in the shade,
And the buttons of his waistcoat bruised my body as he
　　　　clasped me,
Aching, melting, unafraid.
With the shadows of the leaves and the sundrops
And the plopping of the waterdrops,
All about us in the open afternoon —
I am very like to swoon
With the weight of this brocade,
For the sun sifts through the shade.

Underneath the fallen blossom
In my bosom,
Is a letter I have hid.
It was brought to me this morning by a rider from the
　　　　Duke.
"Madam, we regret to inform you that Lord Hartwell
Died in action Thursday se'nnight."
As I read it in the white, morning sunlight,
The letters squirmed like snakes.
"Any answer, Madam?" said my footman.
"No," I told him.
"See that the messenger takes some refreshment.
No, no answer."
And I walked into the garden,
Up and down the patterned paths,

In my stiff, correct brocade.
The blue and yellow flowers stood up proudly in
      the sun,
Each one.
I stood upright too,
Held rigid to the pattern
By the stiffness of my gown.
Up and down I walked,
Up and down.

In a month he would have been my husband.
In a month, here, underneath this lime,
We would have broke the pattern;
He for me, and I for him,
He as Colonel, I as Lady,
On this shady seat.
He had a whim
That sunlight carried blessing.
And I answered, "It shall be as you have said."
Now he is dead.

In Summer and in Winter I shall walk
Up and down
The patterned garden-paths
In my stiff, brocaded gown.
The squills and daffodils
Will give place to pillared roses, and to asters, and
      to snow.

I shall go
Up and down,
In my gown.
Gorgeously arrayed,
Boned and stayed.
And the softness of my body will be guarded
        from embrace
By each button, hook, and lace.
For the man who should loose me is dead,
Fighting with the Duke in Flanders,
In a pattern called a war.
Christ! What are patterns for?

NUMBER 3 ON THE DOCKET

THE lawyer, are you?
Well! I ain't got nothin' to say.
Nothin'!
I told the perlice I hadn't nothin'.
They know'd real well 'twas me.
Ther warn't no supposin',
Ketchin' me in the woods as they did,
An' me in my house dress.
Folks don't walk miles an' miles
In the drifted snow,
With no hat nor wrap on 'em
Ef everythin's all right, I guess.
All right? Ha! Ha! Ha!
Nothin' warn't right with me.
Never was.
Oh, Lord! Why did I do it?
Why ain't it yesterday, and Ed here agin?
Many's the time I've set up with him nights
When he had cramps, or rheumatizm, or somethin'.
I used ter nurse him same's ef he was a baby.
I wouldn't hurt him, I love him!
Don't you dare to say I killed him. 'Twarn't me!
Somethin' got aholt o' me. I couldn't help it.

Oh, what shall I do! What shall I do!
Yes, Sir.
No, Sir.
I beg your pardon, I — I —
Oh, I'm a wicked woman!
An' I'm desolate, desolate!
Why warn't I struck dead or paralyzed
Afore my hands done it.
Oh, my God, what shall I do!
No, Sir, ther ain't no extenuatin' circumstances,
An' I don't want none.
I want a bolt o' lightnin'
To strike me dead right now!
Oh, I'll tell yer.
But it won't make no diff'rence.
Nothin' will.
Yes, I killed him.
Why do yer make me say it?
It's cruel! Cruel!
I killed him because o' th' silence.
The long, long silence,
That watched all around me,
And he wouldn't break it.
I tried to make him,
Time an' agin,
But he was terrible taciturn, Ed was.
He never spoke 'cept when he had to,
An' then he'd only say "yes" and "no."

You can't even guess what that silence was.
I'd hear it whisperin' in my ears,
An' I got frightened, 'twas so thick,
An' al'ays comin' back.
Ef Ed would ha' talked sometimes
It would ha' driven it away;
But he never would.
He didn't hear it same as I did.
You see, Sir,
Our farm was off'n the main road,
And set away back under the mountain;
And the village was seven mile off,
Measurin' after you'd got out o' our lane.
We didn't have no hired man,
'Cept in hayin' time;
An' Dane's place,
That was the nearest,
Was clear way 'tother side the mountain.
They used Marley post-office
An' ours was Benton.
Ther was a cart-track took yer to Dane's in
        Summer,
An' it warn't above two mile that way,
But it warn't never broke out Winters.
I used to dread the Winters.
Seem's ef I couldn't abear to see the golden-
        rod bloomin';
Winter'd come so quick after that.

You don't know what snow's like when yer with it
Day in an' day out.
Ed would be out all day loggin',
An' I set at home and look at the snow
Layin' over everythin';
It 'ud dazzle me blind,
Till it warn't white any more, but black as ink.
Then the quiet 'ud commence rushin' past my ears
Till I most went mad listenin' to it.
Many's the time I've dropped a pan on the floor
Jest to hear it clatter.
I was most frantic when dinner-time come
An' Ed was back from the woods.
I'd ha' give my soul to hear him speak.
But he'd never say a word till I asked him
Did he like the raised biscuits or whatever,
An' then sometimes he'd jest nod his answer.
Then he'd go out agin,
An' I'd watch him from the kitchin winder.
It seemed the woods come marchin' out to meet him
An' the trees 'ud press round him an' hustle him.
I got so I was scared o' th' trees.
I thought they come nearer,
Every day a little nearer,
Closin' up round the house.
I never went in t' th' woods Winters,
Though in Summer I liked 'em well enough.
It warn't so bad when my little boy was with us.

He used to go sleddin' and skatin',
An' every day his father fetched him to school
      in the pung
An' brought him back agin.
We scraped an' scraped fer Neddy,
We wanted him to have a education.
We sent him to High School,
An' then he went up to Boston to Technology.
He was a minin' engineer,
An' doin' real well,
A credit to his bringin' up.
But his very first position ther was an explosion
      in the mine.
And I'm glad! I'm glad!
He ain't here to see me now.
Neddy! Neddy!
I'm your mother still, Neddy.
Don't turn from me like that.
I can't abear it. I can't! I can't!
What did you say?
Oh, yes, Sir.
I'm here.
I'm very sorry,
I don't know what I'm sayin'.
No, Sir,
Not till after Neddy died.
'Twas the next Winter the silence come,
I don't remember noticin' it afore.

That was five year ago,
An' it's been gittin' worse an' worse.
I asked Ed to put in a telephone.
I thought ef I felt the whisperin' comin' **on**
I could ring up some o' th' folks.
But Ed wouldn't hear of it.
He said we'd paid so much for Neddy
We couldn't hardly git along as 'twas.
An' he never understood me wantin' to talk.
Well, this year was worse'n all the others;
We had a terrible spell o' stormy weather,
An' the snow lay so thick
You couldn't see the fences even.
Out o' doors was as flat as the palm o' my **hand,**
Ther warn't a hump or a holler
Fer as you could see.
It was so quiet
The snappin' o' the branches back in the wood-lot
Sounded like pistol shots.
Ed was out all day
Same as usual.
An' it seemed he talked less'n ever.
He didn't even say "Good-mornin'," once or twice,
An' jest nodded or shook his head when I asked **him**
        things.
On Monday he said he'd got to go over to **Benton**
Fer some oats.
I'd oughter ha' gone with him,

But 'twas washin' day
An' I was afeared the fine weather'd break,
An' I couldn't do my dryin'.
All my life I'd done my work punctual,
An' I couldn't fix my conscience
To go junketin' on a washin'-day.
I can't tell you what that day was to me.
It dragged an' dragged,
Fer ther warn't no Ed ter break it in the middle
Fer dinner.
Every time I stopped stirrin' the water
I heerd the whisperin' all about me.
I stopped oftener'n I should
To see ef 'twas still ther,
An' it al'ays was.
An' gittin' louder
It seemed ter me.
Once I threw up the winder to feel the wind.
That seemed most alive somehow.
But the woods looked so kind of menacin'
I closed it quick
An' started to mangle's hard's I could,
The squeakin' was comfortin'.
Well, Ed come home 'bout four.
I seen him down the road,
An' I run out through the shed inter th' barn
To meet him quicker.
I hollered out, "Hullo!"

But he didn't say nothin',
He jest drove right in
An' climbed out o' th' sleigh
An' commenced unharnessin'.
I asked him a heap o' questions;
Who he'd seed
An' what he'd done.
Once in a while he'd nod or shake,
But most o' th' time he didn't do nothin'.
'Twas gittin' dark then,
An' I was in a state,
With the loneliness
An' Ed payin' no attention
Like somethin' warn't livin'.
All of a sudden it come,
I don't know what,
But I jest couldn't stand no more.
It didn't seem's though that was Ed,
An' it didn't seem as though I was me.
I had to break a way out somehow,
Somethin' was closin' in
An' I was stiflin'.
Ed's loggin' axe was ther,
An' I took it.
Oh, my God!
I can't see nothin' else afore me all the time.
I run out inter th' woods,
Seemed as ef they was pullin' me;

An' all the time I was wadin' through the snow
I seen Ed in front of me
Where I'd laid him.
An' I see him now.
There! There!
What you holdin' me fer?
I want ter go to Ed,
He's bleedin'.
Stop holdin' me.
I got to go.
I'm comin', Ed.
I'll be ther in a minit
Oh, I'm so tired!
      (Faints)

THE DOLL

You know, my Dear, I have a way, each Summer
When leaves have changed from ecstasies in green
To something like a crowd with raised umbrellas
Pushing for places at a theatre door,
Whenever there's a reasonable wind —
And when there isn't, why I think it's worse,
They droop so underneath the copper sun
Sitting upon them like a metal cover;
I think the trees look positively tired
Holding the mass of them up all the time.
Well, as I say, when every breeze is smothered
By heavy, lagging leaves on dusty trees,
And all I smell is asphalt and hot tar,
And motor horns destroy the moonlight nights,
I pack myself, and some stray sheets of music,
Into a train and hie me to South Norton.
I came from there, and little drowsy town
Although it is, I still go back (or used to)
And find it with a narrow odd contentment
As grey and glistening as it always was,
Some of it painted, some a silver shimmer
Of weathered clapboards melting to decay. ,
There always is a blaze of Summer flowers
Cramming the dooryards — stocks and portulaca,

And golden glow above the first floor windows,
And China asters mixed with marigolds.
White paint looks very well indeed behind them
And green blinds, always down, you understand,
South Norton people will not risk the daylight
Upon their best room furniture, and really
When you possess an inlaid teak-wood table,
With mother-of-pearl and ebony in squares,
And on it, set precisely in their order,
Stand ivory chess-men, red and white, the queens
A pair of ancient Maharanies copied
To every quaintness of their grand attire
And not a button or embroidery
Skimped by the Hindu carver; when your chairs
Are waxed as never chair is waxed to-day,
And there are corners lit by golden silks,
And mandarin fruit-dishes in high glass cupboards,
Perhaps you may at least be half forgiven
For only opening the room for weddings
Or when some guest from Boston comes to call.
I have called often in such drawing-rooms,
Confused at first by coming from the dazzle
Of a white August sea, and almost groping
To find my hostess in the green-blind dusk,
While all the time my nose was being grateful
For the great puffs of pot-pourri and cloves,
The gusts of myrrh, and sandalwood, and ginger
Invisibly progressing up and down.

These scented rooms are just a paraphrase
Of something penetrant, but never clear,
Never completely taken nor rejected,
Unrealized flotsam of the tides of trade;
And these frail, ancient ladies are like tea-dust
Left in the bottom of a painted chest,
Poor fluttering souls, surrounded by their "things,"
Oblivious of the sea which brought them here.
My Dear, I prose, you really must not let me,
For after all I have something to say.
I never make these duty calls until
My music lessons are a week away
And each day's mail is stuffed with pupils' letters
Asking for dates and prices, then I go
The rounds and drink a dish of tea with each
Old fragile chrysalis and so come home.
For many years I've always ended up
With the two Misses Perkins. They were a whiff
Of eighteen-forty, and I rather liked
To talk to them and then come back and play
Debussy, and thank God I had read Freud;
The contrast was as genial as curry.
I only wish that I could make you see them,
Their garden path with spice-bushes and lilacs,
The scraper by the door, the polished knocker,
And then the hall with the model of a clipper
Upon a table in a square glass case.
She is a replica of the "Flying Dolphin"

And Captain Perkins made her on a voyage
Of eighteen months to China and Ceylon,
Miss Julia just remembers when he brought
The model home and put it where it stands.
I always laid my gloves upon the table
Just by the clipper's stern, and stood my sunshade
Against the corner, and tiptoed up the stairs.
Miss Perkins was an invalid, for years
She had not left her bed, so I was summoned
Up slippery stairs and over cool, long matting
Into her room, and there in a great four-poster
The little lady would greet me with effusion.
"Clara, Dear, how good of you to come,
Julia and I were wondering if you would.
You'll have a cake and a small glass of sherry.
Hannah will bring them in directly. Now
How is the music getting on? To think
You play at concerts! Julia and I read
About your triumphs in the newspapers."
And all the time, behind the house, the sea
Was moving — moving — with a long, slow sound.
I could not hear it, but I clung to it,
For naturally this room looked on the street.
It was a pretty room with bright glazed chintz,
And Naples bay in staring blue gouache,
Flanked by Vesuvius at night, both pictures framed
In peeling gold. Upon the mantelpiece
Were silhouettes: the Captain and his wife,

Miss Perkins and Miss Julia in pantalettes,
A China bear for matches, and a clock
Suspended between alabaster pillars.
But what I never could keep long from seeing
Was a large wax doll, dressed in the Paris fashion
Of sixty years ago, with a lace tippet
And much-flounced skirt over a crinoline,
Upright in a winged arm-chair by the bed.
She sat and gazed with an uncanny ardour
Straight at the andiron, her hands palms upward,
Her feet in heelless slippers wide apart.
She fascinated me. Those blue glass eyes
Had an unearthly meaning, staring straight
Before her in her faded finery.
I had to draw a chair up from the wall,
For never did Miss Perkins or Miss Julia
Suggest that I should sit in the winged chair.
I found my mind all drawn upon a focus,
I thought wax doll and very nearly said so,
And I am very much afraid I missed the point
Of one or two quite artless little sallies.
They never said a word, and I with rigour
Suppressed my curiosity and merely listened
With sometimes half a mind and sometimes none.
I drank the sherry and I eat the cake,
I kissed Miss Perkins when I came to go,
Bending over the bed, my skirt just touching
The doll, I think, and then the call was over.

Of course at first the thing made no impression.
I thought they had been clearing out the attic
And come upon the doll; but when each year
She was still sitting there, I grew to dread
Encountering her, she seemed so full of tales,
Tell-tales of maiden ladies left alone
With still things on the walls and mantelpieces
And nothing moving round them but the sea
Kept out of reach beyond the matted entry.
One year, in early April, coming in
All flushed with having played Moussorgski's "Pictures"
To an enthusiastic audience,
I found a black-edged letter on my table,
Miss Julia writing that "Dear Sister Jane
Had passed away, she wanted me to know."
The words were quaintly quiet and resigned,
The slim and pointed writing very calm,
But still there seemed a wistful hint of dread.
I knew, in fact, Miss Julia was alone.
I wrote — oh, what one always writes, the things
One does not think, and does not want to think.
I sent the letter, and the answer came
As slim, and pointed, and reticent as ever.
And that was all until I reached South Norton.
Of course I went at once to see Miss Julia.
She greeted me beside the clipper-ship,
And there was something grim about that vessel
Placidly sailing on its painted waves

With coffins passing through the door beside it,
From time to time, while nothing ever came.
I wondered what would be its fate, some junk-shop
Probably, when Miss Julia too had gone.
Poor soul, she seemed to flicker with excitement
And sorrow all in one. The great importance
Of doing something which was not commanded
Appeared in vague authoritative gestures
Which seemed but half controlled and faded off
Into a quiver of movement so pathetic
It made me want to cry. She begged me
To go upstairs. "I cannot bear to be
In any other room but Jane's," she told me.
"I've sat there so much with her, quite ten years
It was she did not leave it." So we mounted
The broad old stairs, and softly trod the matting,
Walking gently as in a house of mourning.
I was resentful, it was four full months
Since I had got that lonely little letter.
Was this a mausoleum? Was Miss Julia
To find her only company with ghosts?
The gaudy paper of the narrow hallway,
Flashing its minarets to a sapphire Heaven
Seemed to be mocking us with Eastern splendour,
With Eastern customs and an Eastern languor.
The conch shells roared a siren song of oceans,
Flanking the newel posts, as we passed by them.
Miss Jane's room was a lovely blaze of sunlight,

The empty bed was orderly and sane,
The Bay of Naples gladdened without hurting.
I shook myself free of the swarming stillness
And saw with satisfaction that the chair,
The doll chair, had been moved, it stood beside
The window with its back toward the room.
Why did I walk up to it? I don't know.
Some feeling that the usualness of streets
Comes kindly over a long spent emotion
Perhaps. At any rate, I did so, saying
How bright and gay the portulacas were,
Or something of the sort. And then I started
To sit down in the chair and saw the doll
With palms stretched out and little slippered feet
Pointing before her. There she sat, her eyes
Fixed glassily upon the window-pane.
I may have jumped, at any rate Miss Julia
Flushing a painful pink said steadily:
"It was so dull for her after Jane died,
I moved her here where she could see the street.
It's very comforting to watch the passing,
I think. I always find it so." That's all,
I don't know how the visit went, nor what
I said, nor where I sat. I only know
I took the train that evening back to town
And stayed up half the night playing Stravinsky.
I dreamt wax doll for three weeks afterwards,
And I shall go to London this vacation.

THE DAY THAT WAS THAT DAY

The wind rose, and the wind fell,
And the day that was that day
Floated under a high Heaven.

"Home! Home! Home!"
Sang a robin in a spice-bush.
"Sun on a roof-tree! Sun on a roof-tree!"
Rang thin clouds
In a chord of silver across a placid sky.

Rachel Gibbs stepped up the path
To pass the time of day
With Haywood Green's Minnie.
My, ef she ain't shut th' door!
An' all th' breeze this side th' house too.
She must like to stew.
"Minnie,
Minnie,
You ain't gone out have yer?
I'll skin my knuckles ef I knock agin.
I wonder did she lock th' door —
Well, I never!

Have you gone hard o' hearin'?
Have you —
Minnie, child, what's th' matter?
Why do you look like that?
What you doin'?
Speak I tell yer,
What you hidin' that cup fer?
God A'mighty, girl, what you doin' with wood-alcohol
In a drinkin'-cup?
Here, give it ter me,
An' I'll set it on th' table.
Set down Minnie dear,
Set right here in th' rocker
An' tell me
What ails yer to be wantin'
To drink stuff like that?
There, there, you poor lamb,
Don't look so scared.
Jest tell me all about it,
An' ease your heart.
Minnie, I'll have to shake yer
Ef you don't stop starin'
In that dretful way.
Poor Dear,
You just lay your head up agin me
An' let me soothe yer.
Poor little thing.
Poor little thing."

"Don't, don't, Rachel,
I can't bear it.
I'm a wicked woman,
But I jest couldn't stand no more."

"No more o' what?
Ain't yer Pa good to yer?
What's come over yer, Minnie?
My! I'm jest as sorry as I can be."

"Oh, it ain't nothin' like that.
An' don't be so good to me,
You'll make me want to cry agin,
An' I can't cry.
I'm all dried up,
An' it's like squeezin' my heart sick
To want to cry, an' can't."

"But what is it?
Ain't yer never goin' ter tell me?"

"Why ther' ain't nothin' to tell
'Cept that I'm tired."

"Now, look-a-here, Minnie,
No one don't drink poison jest 'cause they're tired."

"I didn't drink it, as it happens."

"No, you didn't, 'cause I come in an' stopped yer.
But I'm mighty afeered you would have.
Lord, it makes me shudder!"

"I guess yer right,
I would have.
An' I wish you'd ha' let me be.
Now it's all to do over agin,
An' I don't know as I'll git th' courage
A second time.
I guess you ain't never been right down tired, Rachel."

"Well, never to th' poison point, no, I haven't
But what's gone wrong to wear yer out so?"

"The cat's sick."

"Minnie Green, was you takin' poison
'Cause you got a sick cat?
That's down-right foolishness."

"Yes, it does sound so.
But I couldn't face nussin' her.
Look here, Rachel,
I may be foolish, or mad, or jest plain bad,
But I couldn't stan' another thing.
I'm all fretted now

An' more's one too many.
I can't go on!
Oh, God! I can't go on!
I ain't got no more'n most women,
I know that,
But I fuss a lot more.
There's al'ays th' same things
Goin' roun' like th' spokes to a cart-wheel,
Ef one ain't a-top it's another,
An' th' next comin' up all th' time.
It's breakfast, an' dinner, an' supper,
Every day.
An' th' same dishes to wash.
I hate them dishes.
I smashed a plate yesterday
'Cause I couldn't bear to see it
Settin' on th' sink waitin' fer me.
An' when I go up to make Father's bed
I get seasick
Thinkin' I'll have to see that old check spread agin.
I've settled it,
An' twitched it this way an' that,
For thirty year,
An' I hate th' sight o' th' thing.
Sometimes I've set an hour on th' stair
Ruther'n go in an' touch it.
Oh my God! Why couldn't yer let me be?
Why'd you have to come interferin'?

Why?
Why?"

"Thank th' Everlastin' Mercy I did!
But, Minnie, how long's this been goin' on?
I never had no idea anythin' was wrong."

"I don't know.
For ever an' ever, I guess.
Rachel, you can't think how hard it is fer me
To set one foot after th' other sometimes.
I hate lookin' out th' winder,
I'm so tired o' seein' th' path to th' barn.
An' I can't hardly bear
To hear father talkin' to th' horses.
He loves 'em.
But I don't love nothin'
'Cept th' cat,
An' cats is cold things to cling to,
An' now mine's sick!"

"Don't take on so, Minnie.
She'll get well.
There, you rest awhile
You can tell me afterwards."

A wind rose, and a wind fell,
And the day that was that day
Hung against a turning sun.

The robin sang "Home! Home! Home!"
In an up-and-down scale of small, bright notes.
The clouds rang silver arpeggios
Stretched across a pleasant sky.

"I wish I loved somethin', Rachel."

"Bless your heart, Child, don't you love yer Father?"

"I suppose so. But he don't mean nothin' ter me.
He don't say nothin' I want ter hear.
My ears is achin' to hear words,
Words like what's written in books,
Words that would make me all bright like a Spring
         day.
I lay awake nights
Thinkin' o' hearin' things,
An' seein' things.
I'm awful tired o' these hills,
They crowd in so.
Seems sometimes ef I could see th' ocean,
Or a real big city,
'Twould help.
Kind o' lay my eyes out straight fer a while,
Everythin's so short here
My eyes feels pushed in,
An' it hurts 'em.

I love laylocks,
But I git so tired o' watchin'
Th' leaves come an' th' flowers
Every year th' same,
I'd like to root 'em up.
I've set an' set in th' kitchen evenin's
Awful late,
Fer not bein' able to git up an' light th' lamp
To go ter bed.
I'm all lead somehow.
I guess ef anybody did say anythin'
I'd be deaf
Jest with listenin' so long.
I'm plumb tired out."

"Look-a-here, Minnie,
Why don't you go away
Fer a spell?"

"Me go away!
Oh, no, I couldn't never do that.
I couldn't go no place.
I can't hardly git over to Dicksville
Fer my week with Aunt Abby now.
I'm all wrong away from home.
I can't do nothin'!
Nothin' at all.
I'm so awful tired."

"Minnie, did you ever love anybody?
Any man, I mean?"

"No, Rachel, I never did.
I know that sounds queer, but it's a fact.
I've tried to think I did,
But 'twarn't true.
I hadn't hardly no time fer men-folks,
Mother was sick so long,   .
An' then ther' was Father.
I never was much account with 'em anyway,
But I s'pose I might ha' had one
Ef I'd fixed my mind so.
But I al'ays waited.
An' now I'm through waitin',
I'm through waitin' fer anythin', Rachel.
It's jest go, go, go,
With never no end,
And nothin' done that ain't to do over agin.
Ther' now it's six o'clock,
An' I must be gittin' supper.
You needn't move that cup, Rachel.
I ain't a-goin' to touch it.
I'll jest keep on now till th' Lord takes me
An' I only hope he'll do it soon."

The robin flew down from the spice-bush

And pecked about for worms.
The clouds were brazen trumpets
Tumbled along the edge of an apple-coloured sky.
The shadow of the house
Fell across the path to the barn
Confusing it with the grass and the daisies.

A wind rose, and a wind fell,
And the day that was that day
Vanished in the darkness.

THE ROSEBUD WALL-PAPER

So you been peekin' int' th' winders o' th' old porch
      house to th' Four Corners,

Have ye?

Wall, I dunno as anybody wouldn't be puzzled

Not knowin' nothin' 'bout it, an' seein' it th' way 'tis.

I bet you had a time pushin' through them cat-briers

That's growed up all about it.

Terrible stiff bushes they be, an' th' scratchiest things
      goin'.

Oh, you needn't tell me!

Many's th' first-class tear I've got from 'em in my
      time.

Not those pertic'ler ones, I ain't no call to go shovin'
      through them,

An' what on earth you wanted to tackle 'em for beats
      me.

But, since you been ther',

It's just nater you should want to know.

A house all sagged down an' rotted, an' th' chimbley
      fell,

An' every room spick an' span with new wall-paper!

Sort o' creepy, was it?

I guess th' creeps is ther' all right,

But we figgered we'd smothered 'em with that rosebud
  paper.
Mrs. Pearson, th' doctor's wife, had th' choosin' of it.
She went to Boston a-purpose when th' town decided to
  put it on.
I al'ays thought 'twas kind o' gay for what they wanted
  it for,
But Mrs. Pearson said it had ought to be gay
An' she's a real tasty woman;
Nobody darsn't go agin her judgment in this town,
Least of all th' selectmen with th' doctor chairman o'
  th' board.
Well, Mr. Day, ther's a good long story to that wall-
  paper.
Th' beginnin's way back, all of thirty year, I guess.
Ther' was a storekeeper here at that time, name o'
  Amos Sears.
He warn't a native o' th' place,
I've heerd he come from somewheres down Cape Cod
  way,
He just sort o' drifted here an' stuck.
His wife was dead, an' he had a son, young Amos,
Who used to play around with us boys.
You know what boys be, al'ays in an' out o' one an-
  other's pockets.
Young Amos was a fine, upstandin' chap.
We all favoured him, but he an' Luke Bartlett was like
  a plum an' its skin,

You couldn't peel 'em apart.

They beat th' band for mischief an' high jinks,

Th' rest of us just follered along an' caught th'
     lickin's.

'Bout th' time we was gittin' through school, old Amos
     died.

We thought, o' course, young Amos'd settle right down
     to th' shop,

But he wouldn't hear to it, said he couldn't rest quiet
     without he'd done a bit o' trapesin'

Afore he took root for keeps;

An' first thing we knew, he'd hired Tom Wetherbee to
     look after th' business

An' was off.

He wanted Luke should go with him,

But Luke was a real steady youngster, he'd 'prenticed
     himself to a stone-mason

An' wouldn't budge.

I guess now he wishes some he'd gone,

But I dunno, 'tain't easy seein' into other folks' minds.

I went studyin' surveyin' to Barre

An' warn't here when Amos left.

Luke heerd from him two or three times,

But pretty soon th' letters stopped.

Tom Wetherbee went on 'tendin' to th' shop

An' payin' his own wages out o' th' earnin's.

What he didn't need for repairin' an' to keep th' stock
     up, he put in th' bank for Amos,

But Amos never drawed any of it,
So it just piled up.
What Amos lived on, I dunno, he never told nobody to
     my knowledge.
But he lived somehow, an' after ten years
He come back with a wife.
Mrs. Amos was a fine figger of a woman,
With eyes like steel traps, an' a tongue like a mowin'
     machine.
She al'ays reminded me of a sumach when it's turned in
     th' Autumn,
Sort o' harsh an' bright. You couldn't see nothin' else
When she was around, but she warn't th' easy kind,
Her nerves was like a bundle o' fire-crackers,
An' it didn't take no slow-match to light 'em.
She could do anythin' she set her hand to,
But she made such a touse doin' it
You'd full as lives not have it done.
Amos found quite a bit o' money waitin' for him in th'
     Wiltshire bank,
An' he found th' store in extra good shape,
So th' first thing he done was to buy a house.
Not th' one you see, that didn't come till later,
Th' third house from th' post-office was his.
Then he took Tom Wetherbee into partnership
An' moved into his new house, an' things begun.
They begun with a vengeance, but we didn't know
     nothin' for some time.

Th' house, maybe you noticed, stands quite a piece
    above th' road.

Did you see anythin' queer 'bout th' grass either side
    th' steps?

Well, that was 'cause Amos an' Mrs. couldn't come
    to no agreement 'bout fixin' up th' lawn.

He set by a straight slope an' she wanted terraces,

So they had a straight slope to one side an' terraces to th'
    other.

Amos made a joke of it, but Mrs. Amos she made a
    grievance;

She made most everythin' a grievance.

She was al'ays runnin' roun' an' tattlin' aginst Amos.

I expect she had one o' them tongues they say's hung in
    th' middle;

If one end got tired, all she had to do was let it be an' go
    right along with th' other.

When she warn't scoldin' Amos, she was scoldin' 'bout
    him.

But in th' end 'twarn't him as give, 'twas her.

She up an' runned away, boarded th' afternoon train to
    Boston

One day while he was mindin' th' shop.

When Amos found out she'd gone

He got Bill Rivers (Rivers kep' th' livery stable then) to
    hitch up his Morgan mare in a couple o' shakes

An' drive him over to th' junction, lickety split, to ketch
    th' night train from Fitchburg.

He ketched it all right, but 'twas nip an' tuck,
Th' conductor was hollerin' "All aboard!" when they
come in sight o' th' depot.
I mind Rivers was some put out 'cause Amos didn't say
a single word
All th' way over,
Didn't even think to thank him when he got him ther'.
Amos was back in a little over a week,
But he didn't bring Mrs. Amos with him.
Luke went up to see him right away,
An' he told Luke Mrs. Amos had gone for a stewardess
on a Halifax steamboat.
She had th' sea in her blood, he said,
An' he guessed she couldn't be happy livin' so far from
it.
It seems she was a New Bedford woman,
An' all her folks had been whalers.
Everybody supposed as how Amos would sell his house
an' shop
An' go an' settle somewheres his wife would like.
But he didn't do no such thing.
He just hung on, lookin' as gloomy as a rainy Fourth o'
July;
An' he kep' a-hangin', neither here nor ther' exactly,
He didn't seem fixed to stay, an' he didn't go.
Things went on like that for more'n a year,
An' then Amos bought that parcel o' land to th' Four
Corners, an' put up th' house you see.

When 'twas finished, he sold th' old house an' moved in.
He druv into town every day to th' store,
But folks didn't go out to see him.
He'd turned terr'ble glum an' pernickety
An' Luke was th' only man on real terms with him.
You couldn't git anythin' out o' Luke,
He was mum as a fish,
That's how we didn't come to hear 'bout Mrs. Richards
        bein' with Amos
Till she'd been ther' quite a spell.
I dunno's we'd ever have heerd but for Bill Rivers driv-
        in' some Summer boarders
Up Hog Back one August afternoon.
One o' th' ladies had a faintin' fit or somethin',
An' Rivers stopped to Amos's to ask if she couldn't rest
        ther' while th' others went on.
He was took all aback when Mrs. Richards come out.
Rivers was a awful talker,
He'd twist a bit o' news under his tongue same as if 'twas
        a chaw o' tobaccer
An' I never see a man take such relish in spreadin' it.
So th' whole town knowed 'bout Mrs. Richards 'fore
        he'd been back an hour.
You know how folks be, once git a story started
An' it's off rampagin' like a forest fire.
Somebody said Luke'd know, an' two or three went up
        to Luke's
An' asked him.

But Luke just said "Why not? Amos had to have some
    one to do for him,

An' Mrs. Richards was a respectable widow from Mill-
    bridge."

Ther' warn't no gainsayin' that, when Luke pointed it
    out,

But what folks don't say ain't al'ays a handle to what
    they thinks.

Luke was a real smart man, an' he wouldn't listen to a
    word aginst her an' Amos,

An' nobody darsn't say a thing to Amos himself nat'r-
    ally.

So it went on. Amos had a hired housekeeper, said Luke;

Amos had somethin' he shouldn't have had, said others.

But that was only hearsay, an' Mrs. Richards' husband
    had been th' postmaster to Millbridge for years

Until he'd been took off by th' pneumony three years
    before,

An' left nothin'.

"So his widow had to work," said Luke's friends.

Amos's friends didn't say nothin' seein' he didn't rightly
    have any,

Barrin' Luke, but that was enough.

Luke was a powerful perseverin' man, an' wouldn't
    stand no nonsense.

But, spite o' Luke, ther' was talk, heaps of it.

You can't keep women from enjoyin' a story like that,

Nor men neither, I guess.

A good few o' th' boys went out to Amos's
An' they telled how cozy 'twas out ther',
With white curtings to th' winders
An' th' chiny on th' dresser all set out elegant,
Nothin' out o' place an' a sort o' cheery look to every-
    thin'.
Amos had planted apple-trees an' they was just come to
    bear.
Early sugar apples they was, you know th' kind,
Yaller streaked with red an' sweet as honey.
To hear th' talk you'd think no one else in th' town
Had apples. Boys will be boys, even when they ain't,
An' ther' was somethin' 'bout Mrs. Richards menfolk
    couldn't have enough of.
But Amos didn't turn a hair, he know'd his woman.
'Twas al'ays th' same — apples, an' cookies, an' black-
    berry jam, an' a welcome.
Amos warn't like th' same man he was to th' store,
He'd laugh an' joke, for all th' world like he used to do
    in th' old days,
'Twas good to hear him.
Th' women didn't go, though I guess they was itchin' to,
But none on 'em darst begin.
Women is sticklers for custom,
An' all that whisperin' made a sort o' fence
They couldn't break through.
I've sometimes wondered if that ain't th' real use o'
    women,

To keep things goin' on even an' straight, with no
    bumps an' jumps to onsettle ye.
O' course ther's th' other kind o' women, th' Mrs. Amos
    kind,
But, praise th' Lord, I ain't had much to do with them.
But, however stiddy they be, women is terr'ble cur'ous
    critters,
They can't git along without a deal o' worritin' 'bout th'
    neighbours' concerns.
An' I do believe our Parson's wife was th' most cur'ous
    woman ever was.
She was at th' Parson from mornin' till night to go out
    to Amos's.
You see she wanted to know how things was at first
    hand,
But she know'd better'n to say so.
What she said was that his duty called him to go an' see
    if Amos was a errin' man;
If he kep' a scarlet woman to th' Corners, th' Parson
    ought to try an' git him away from her
An' save his soul.
'Twas a bitter strong argiment to use to a Parson,
An' she used it every day an' all day.
'Twas clear he wouldn't git no peace till he went,
An' Parson Eldridge loved peace.
He was a meek little man
An' didn't hold with pokin' in wher' 'twarn't agreeable,
But he had to go, an' he did.

Mrs. Eldridge must have been mortal disappointed,
For all he said when he come back was
That Amos didn't appear to be livin' in sin.
He didn't say he warn't, mind you,
But he 'lowed to his wife he couldn't see no openin' to
      start savin' his soul.
"Th' Almighty works in his own ways," he said,
"An' Amos has had a heavy cross to bear."
He didn't name no names, but it set us all to thinkin' o'
      Mrs. Amos
An' what a dance she'd led Amos.
It made us feel sorry for him,
An' after that we kind o' sidelooked his failin'
If so be as 'twas one,
An' th' tittle tattle an' speculatin' died down.
Also we was gittin' used to things, I guess.
Well, they kep' that way for a good fifteen year
An' then one night Amos called th' doctor on th' tele-
      phone.
His voice was gritty an' shakin', so th' doctor said after-
      wards,
An' he know'd at once somethin' had happened.
Mrs. Richards was real bad, Amos said,
Could th' doctor come right away.
So Dr. Pearson got out his flivver an' started for th'
      Corners.
'Twas just commencin' to snow, but 'twarn't so deep th'
      car couldn't run,

Nor it warn't so light it didn't matter.

'Twas one o' them stingin' snow-storms,

With th' flakes so little you can't hardly see 'em

But drivin' with a awful force.

That kind o' snow don't seem to lay none at first,

But ther' ain't no melt to it, an' it goes on an' on,

Comin' every way to oncet, an' blowin' up into drifts
   which you can't make out wher' they be or ain't
   till you're on 'em.

One side th' road'll be swep' clear,

An' th' other all piled up with snow higher'n your head,

An' all th' time you're as good as blind

'Count o' th' flakes bein' so sharp an' sheddin' down so
   almighty fast.

Some men wouldn't have gone out,

Dr. Blake to Millbridge wouldn't, I know,

But Dr. Pearson went wher' he was needed;

Battle an' murder an' suddin death couldn't stop him if
   any one was sick.

It took him all of an hour to git to th' Corners,

An' he know'd when he got ther' he couldn't git back.

Amos met him at th' door,

"I mistake but you're too late, Doctor," says he.

And so 'twas. Mrs. Richards was dead.

She'd had a heart attack, and died while th' doctor was
   on his way.

Th' doctor done what he could just to comfort Amos by
   doin' somethin',

But in th' end he had to tell him 'twas all over.

Then th' doctor was scared, Amos acted so queer.

He turned as white as marble, an' as stiff.

He stood ther', lookin' down at th' bed,

Lookin' with his eyes like stones o' fire,

Froze an' burnin' at th' same time.

He never moved 'em from th' dead face,

Just stared still as ice, as if he was all shelled in it,

But somethin' hot an' hard was scaldin' him inside.

Th' doctor tried to rouse him, but he didn't seem to
   hear.

Then th' doctor took his hand an' raised it up,

But when he let it go, it fell down by his side agin,

An' Amos didn't seem to notice that he'd took it an'
   dropped it.

Dr. Pearson couldn't leave him ther' alone,

An' he couldn't go anyway 'cause o' th' storm.

Th' snow kep' risin' higher an' higher on th' winders.

Th' door was clean blocked, an' when mornin' come

Th' doctor couldn't see his car, 'twas all buried in.

All night long Amos had stood just th' same way

Starin' at th' dead woman.

He might have been dead himself, or a moniment.

He didn't give a sign he was livin',

Only ther' was mist on a hand-glass th' doctor held to
   his mouth.

Th' doctor tried to force some coffee down his throat,

But his jaw was clinched an' he couldn't prize it open.

He tried to throw him over so's he could git him layin'
down,

But he couldn't budge him no more'n if he'd been a
granite boulder.

Seem's he had th' stren'th o' ten men

Just to keep standin' ther' lookin' at that dead body,

'Twas a Sunday night Amos called th' doctor,

An' 'twas Wednesday mornin' afore th' storm broke.

An' all that time Amos had stood ther' without movin'
a muscle,

Only he'd sort o' shrunk together; not stoopin', I don't
mean,

But collapsin' in sideways.

Th' doctor put it he looked brittle

Like you might snap him in two but couldn't overset
him nohow.

Maybe 'twas th' sunlight done it. The sun shone
straight in his eyes,

But he never even winked 'em, just kep' on lookin' an'
lookin'.

'Bout 'leven o'clock a sleigh come for th' doctor.

They'd been tryin' to git to him for two days

But couldn't, th' drifts was so high,

They'd had to shovel most o' th' way as 'twas.

When th' doctor let 'em in ('twas th' two Fowler boys
an' Sam Gould)

Th' first thing he told 'em was to come upstairs an' help
him with Amos.

But they hadn't hardly set foot in th' room

When Amos tumbled over on th' floor — same as a tree,
    they said,

Stiff from head to foot, not limp like a man in a
    faint.

Th' boys picked him up an' laid him on th' bed in th'
    next room,

An' th' doctor worked over him; but 'twas hours 'fore
    he give a sign o' life,

An' when he did, he went right out of his head with
    fever.

He warn't sensible for some days, an' by that time th'
    funeral was over an' done with.

They telled him how 'twas when they thought he could
    stand it,

But he didn't seem to care,

I guess he'd buried her in his mind long before,

Durin' th' storm.

Folks was awful sorry for Amos,

But he didn't act to take much stock in that neither.

He got up an' went about,

But he didn't go to th' store no more,

An' he didn't take no steps to git a new housekeeper.

Mrs. Eldridge had a string o' middle-aged women to
    suggest for th' place,

But th' Parson kep' her off him somehow.

I al'ays had a likin' for th' Parson after that;

Maybe he'd sensed more'n we thought, all along.

He was a good man, too good to go interferin' with th'
  Almighty's doin's,
An' that's what you can't say o' most parsons.
Come Spring, one afternoon when Luke Bartlett was
  workin' in his yard,
Tinkerin' at a funeral urn for Elder Townsend's moni-
  ment,
Who should come creepin' in but Amos Sears.
Luke was all took aback seein' him comin' in so quiet,
Almost stealin' in, you might say,
'Cause Amos had shown him pretty plain that he didn't
  set nothin' by seein' him.
Luke was a sensitive man, an' Amos turnin' from him
  had hurt him dretful.
Amos crep' up to him, peerin' as if he couldn't see very
  well,
An' hangin' onto his stick like 'twas a third leg he
  couldn't do without.
"Luke," says he, "Luke, we been old friends, you an'
  me."
"We have, Amos," says Luke.
"Luke," says Amos agin, "I've had a sight to bear in
  my life."
"You have, Amos," says Luke.
"'Tis you, Luke, an' you only can ease me now, if you
  will," says Amos, an' ther' was tears in his eyes.
Luke seen 'em an' they made him feel sick all over,
Amos warn't one to cry.

Now what do you s'pose it was he wanted Luke should
do?

Why, make a gravestone for Mrs. Richards, an' that
was all ther' was to it.

Everythin' went slick as paint till they come to th' inscription;

Amos had that all writ out nice on a piece of paper

An' he read it to Luke.

"Here lies th' body o' Mary Richards,

Beloved friend an' onlawful wife o' Amos Sears,

For seventeen years his sole comfort by th' grace o' God.

Blessed be th' name of th' Lord whose ways are inscrut-
able.

Erected by her bereaved husband in th' sight o' Heaven
wher' ther's no marriage nor givin' in marriage,

But joyful meetin' without end for ever an' ever. Amen."

Luke took th' paper when Amos handed it to him,

But he couldn't git aholt o' no words quick enough to
speak 'em.

Maybe he'd know'd al'ays, same as Parson Eldridge,

Maybe he'd thought what he said he did.

But anyways you look at it that inscription was a
baffler.

Here was Amos givin' himself away to th' whole town.

He put it to him so, but Amos said he wouldn't keep it
hid no more,

That 'twas like th' burnin' bush to him,

Th' love they'd bore each other.

Then Luke argid 'twas sacrilege to ask th' blessin' o' th'
      Lord for a onsanctified union.

"Who says 'twarn't sanctified," shouted Amos,

"She was th' Lord's givin' to lighten th' sorrow He'd set
      so heavy on me.

God's just, as I've heerd from th' pulpit many a time,

An' I don't cal'ate you're denyin' it,

An' He done th' square thing by me.

I'd be a limpin' coward if I didn't proclaim it to all an'
      sundry,

Witness as I be to His mercy an' comprehendin' kind-
      ness."

That was too much for Luke. He was a Godfearin'
      man,

An' he thought Amos had gone blasphemin' crazy.

But Amos hadn't, not then.

They went at it, hammer an' tongs,

Each talkin' nineteen to th' dozen.

Then th' pity of it come over Luke,

An' he said he'd try to see it Amos's way

An' tell him in a month when th' stone'd be near done.

An' Amos had to do with that for th' time bein'.

Luke made th' gravestone just as Amos said,

Of good black slate, with th' top poked up in a little
      round just big enough for a angel's head,

An' th' wings reachin' out right an' left underneath —

Luke had a won'erful knack with angels, he put on most
      all his stones —

But when it come to th' inscription, he couldn't stomach
it.

So he just put "Here lies Mary Richards. God's will be
done."

He'd worked it out that them words'd fit most anythin'
an' they wouldn't shock nobody.

If Amos was right 'bout th' Almighty's designin's,
they'd mean that,

An' if he warn't, they'd mean otherwise. They'd come
in handy either way.

Then he went an' set it up himself,

I guess he was kind o' afeared Amos might break it or
somethin'.

Well, th' month was up by then, an' he had to give his
answer to Amos.

I dessay he didn't look forward to it any,

But Luke warn't th' man to shirk a duty,

An' that very evenin', soon's supper was over, he started
for th' Corners.

Luke never telled what happened that night, but I know
for a fact that him an' Amos never spoke agin.

Ther' warn't much time for speakin', as a matter o' fact,

For 'twas th' next Tuesday I went up to th' graveyard.

I don't mind now why, I hadn't buried none o' my folks
for years,

But I did go up, an' wandered round for a spell,

An' all of a suddin I come on Mrs. Richards' grave.

I didn't know nothin' 'bout th' inscription,

Luke didn't say anythin' 'bout it till 'twas all over,

So 'twarn't that made me look at th' stone.

Then I couldn't scarcely b'lieve my eyes,

Th' stone was all writ over with red letters.

First I thought they was blood,

But then I see they was red chalk runnin' straight between th' lines Luke had cut.

Yes, Sir, you've guessed it. 'Twas Amos's inscription,

Fixed so's to read right along with Luke's;

An' Luke's letters was chalked too, it looked all of a
  piece a little ways off.

Thinks I, th' man who could do that must be goin'
  through blazes,

His grievin' must have plumb crazed him,

I guess 'twould be a Christian act to go an' see how he
  be.

I warn't anxious for goin', but I didn't see how any decent man

Could leave them letters an' just go off home.

I'll never forget that drive to th' Corners, never.

Every tree I passed looked so's I'd never seen it till that
  minit,

They stuck out at me an' made me notice 'em,

I can almost tell you how many leaves ther' was to every
  branch.

An' ther' was th' Ford chuggin' away,

An' th' thrushes singin' their sunset songs,

An' th' sun goin' down behind Hog Back.

My! How black th' mountain was with th' sky turnin'
all kinds o' colours behind it,

An' th' air comin' cool an' damp when we struck th'
shadow o' th' mountain!

'Twas all shadow to Amos's, but back yonder t'other
side o' th' valley was full o' sun,

It holds a good hour longer down ther'.

I jumped out o' th' car an' knocked on th' door,

But nobody answered.

Then I done th' same as you did, I peeked int' th' winders.

But I couldn't see if Amos was inside or not.

In th' end I just made bold an' opened th' door.

Red chalk, did I say?

Red, an' white, an' green, an' blue, an' purple chalk!

'Twas chalk, chalk, all roun' th' room!

An' 'twas ships done with chalk!

Ther' was a steamboat fightin' waves as tall as th' fun-
nels,

Roarin' over her they was, with a noise like artil'ry,

I swear I heerd 'em, an' I sensed she'd be swamped in a
minit.

'Twas a rackin' thing to watch her strugglin' to keep up

With no more chance than a fly under a pump spout.

An' another steamboat (they was all steamboats) runnin' on rocks, black rocks, with red an' green
waves dashin' th' ship onto 'em.

Th' next was th' ship goin' to pieces,

An' th' waves was all full o' people clingin' to bits of
wood.

Some was hangin' on a little longer, some was drownin'
as you looked.

I can't describe how awful 'twas.

One ship was afire, with great tongues o' yaller flame
bustin' through black smoke.

Not another vessel was near, just th' heavin' sea wal-
lowin' in th' glitter o' th' flames.

Ther' was a steamer struck by a bolt o' lightnin',

Riv' clear down th' middle, an' th' crew was takin' to th'
life-boats,

An' th' life-boats was over-loaded an' sinkin' as fast as
they was launched.

I was cold all over with lookin' 'fore I come to th' last,

An' that was th' worst of all.

'Twas a dismasted hulk driftin' with th' run o' th' waves,

Only ther' warn't no waves, th' ocean was calm,

So calm it made you want to scream.

Dawn was comin', an' th' light was just showin' that
ther' was a ocean at all,

But 'twarn't no good to see it for ther' warn't nothin'
to see but it.

'Twas done pretty big, an' you could make out ther'
was somebody on th' ship,

An' that 'twas a woman.

Somehow you know'd she was all th' folks ther' was,

An' th' hulk had drifted out o' th' way o' other ships,

An' that 'twas just goin' to float along like that with th'
     woman on it
Till th' food give out an' she died o' starvation.
By that time I was in a sweat all over.
There was a lonesomeness an' a downright nastiness
     'bout them picters
I can't describe to ye,
But you'd have felt it too, if you'd seen 'em.
I'm glad you didn't, I wouldn't wish any one to be
     haunted by 'em same as I been.
I'd just finished an' was startin' all over agin 'cause I
     couldn't keep from it,
When Amos come in.
"You didn't know I could do nothin' like that, did
     you?" says Amos,
Beginnin' in th' middle, with not so much as a "How
     d'you do" to set things goin'.
"No," says I, "I didn't. Be these your doin'?"
"They be," says he. "I'm pretty smart at drawin' now.
I guess ther's more in a man than he knows till he
     tries."
I didn't answer, not findin' what to say,
But he didn't notice that.
"I been at it all Winter," he says,
"Quick as I worked out a new way for th' sea to kill
I slapped it down on th' wall yonder.
I guess I ain't left out a single one; if I learn I have, I'll
     put it on th' ceilin'.

Curse that woman! One on 'em must strike!

Th' sea's so notional at killin' 'twon't leave her be much
       longer,

Stan's to reason she's nearin' her term.

Eighteen year she's been at it, temptin' it an' floutin' it

Same's she's flouted me.

Th' sea won't desert me th' way Luke done,

Th' sea'll be my friend.

Ain't I prayed to it every night an' mornin'

To git her quick.

I shall go mad 'fore long if somethin' don't happen.

Joshua" — an' he grabbed my arm — "you think it'll
       git her pretty soon, don't ye?"

I was scared, Mr. Day, scared to hear him sayin' such
       things.

He was tremblin' from head to foot, an' his eyes had a
       mean, dry look in 'em

I'd never see in nobody's.

"Amos," I says, "be you speakin' o' your wife?"

"You tarnation fool!" says he, droppin' my arm an'
       ragin' off roun' th' room,

"Of course I be. If I warn't a God damn coward, I'd
       kill her with my own hands.

But th' sea's my depity; I've appointed it in my place,
       an' I'm just waitin' for news.

An' I'll wait till Hog Back's a valley, an' don't you go
       doubtin' it."

I didn't doubt, I was beginnin' to know Amos,

But what he said riled me so, I couldn't keep from hollerin' out:

"God in Heaven, man, don't you know she was
drownded in a wreck two year ago!"

'Twarn't right to tell him like that, an' I was ashamed
to th' marrer at what I'd done th' minit after,

For Amos went down as if he'd been shot.

You see, Mr. Day, he couldn't git a devorce

'Count o' havin' signed a paper agreein' to a separation
when his wife left him,

An' that queered his case accordin' to law.

An' here he might ha' been married to Mrs. Richards
for two years anyway,

If he'd ha' know'd.

I can't think how he didn't, 'cept that 'twas in a Port-
land paper I read it

One time when I was down that way.

'Twas enough to upset any man comin' on him suddin
like that,

But I warn't prepared for his way o' takin' it.

I hadn't had time to think o' th' half o' what I'm tellin'
you

When he was up an' runnin' at me with a chair.

"Get out!" he screamed, "you get out or I'll smash you
into hell."

Chair for chair, I was no match for him,

It was just dodge an' run for me.

When I got to the door I made a dash for it,

An' I'd just got my car goin' when he reached me,

But a motor on high ain't a thing to fool with

An' I got away.

I druv for all th' car was worth to Parson Eldridge's

An' telled him th' whole story.

He got a posse o' men together an' off we all went back
        to Amos's.

But we couldn't find him anywheres about th' place.

Parties searched th' woods, and th' ponds was dragged

But we never come on a thing, not till this day.

Nobody knows if he's dead or livin'.

All th' towns for miles was notified,

But he warn't never found,

No one ain't ever see hair or hide of him since that
        day.

That was six Summers come next,

An' anybody you don't know's dead ain't lawfully
        such for I don't know how many years,

So nothin' couldn't be done with his effects.

Ther' stood th' house an' them fearsome picters

Any one could see 'em through th' winders if they was
        lookin' for 'em,

An' they was scary as I can't tell ye.

It got to be a dare with th' little fellers to go out an'
        peek,

An' some o' th' boys couldn't sleep nights for 'em.

After John Baxter's youngest screamed himself into
        fits,

Th' selectmen took it on themselves to order th' walls
  papered.

'Twouldn't injure his property none to put it on, they
  'lowed,

He could rip it off when he come back, if he'd a mind to.

Th' house must ha' been jerrybuilt to have fell away
  so in th' time,

But that was kind o' like Amos's life, warn't it?

'Twas jerrybuilt clear through, I guess.

But you just thank your stars for them rosebuds, that's
  all.

HEDGE ISLAND

A Retrospect and a Prophecy

Hedges of England, peppered with sloes; hedges of England, rows and rows of thorn and brier raying out from the fire where London burns with its steaming lights, throwing a glare on the sky o' nights. Hedges of England, road after road, lane after lane, and on again to the sea at the North, to the sea at the East, blackberry hedges, and man and beast plod and trot and gallop between hedges of England, clipped and clean; beech, and laurel, and hornbeam, and yew, wheels whirl under, and circle through, tunnels of green to the sea at the South; wind-blown hedges to mark the mouth of Thames or Humber, the Western rim. Star-point hedges, smooth and trim.

Star-point indeed, with all His Majesty's mails agog every night for the provinces. Twenty-seven fine crimson coaches drawn up in double file in Lombard Street. Great gold-starred coaches, blazing with royal insignia, waiting in line at the Post-Office. Eight of a Summer's evening, and the sun only just gone down. "Lincoln," "Winchester," "Portsmouth," shouted from the Post-Office steps; and the Portsmouth chestnuts come up to the collar with a jolt, and stop again, dancing, as the bags are hoisted up. "Gloucester," "Oxford," "Bristol," "York," "Norwich." Rein in those bays of the Norwich team, they shy badly at the fangleam of the lamp over the Post-Office door. "All in. No more." The stones of St. Martin's-le-Grand sparkle under the slap of iron shoes. Off you go, bays, and the greys of the Dover mail start forward, twitching, hitching, champing, stamping, their little feet pat the ground in patterns and their bits fleck foam. "Whoa! Steady!" with a rush they are gone. But Glasgow is ready with a team of piebalds and sorrels, driven chess-board fashion. Bang down, lids of mail-boxes — thunder-lids, making the horses start. They part and pull, push each other sideways, sprawl on the slippery pavement, and gather wave-like and crashing to a leap. Spicey tits those! Tootle-too! A nice calculation for the gate, not a minute to spare, with the wheelers well up in the bit and the leaders carrying bar. Forty-two hours to Scotland, and we have a coachman who keeps his horses like clock-work. Whips flick, buckles click, and wheels turn faster and faster till the spokes blur. "Sound your horn, Walter." Make it echo back and forth from the fronts of houses. Good-night, London, we are carrying the mails to the North. Big, burning light which is London, we dip over Highgate hill and leave you. The air is steady, the night is bright, the roads are firm. The wheels hum like a gigantic spinning-jenny. Up North, where the hedges bloom with roses. Through Whet-

stone Gate to Alconbury Hill. Stop at the *Wheatsheaf*
one minute for the change. They always have an eye
open here, it takes thirty seconds to drink a pot of beer,
even the post-boys sleep in their spurs. The wheels purr
over the gravel. "Give the off-hand leader a cut on the
cheek." Whip! Whew! This is the first night of three.
Three nights to Glasgow; hedges — hedges — shoot and
flow. Eleven miles an hour, and the hedges are showered
with glow-worms. The hedges and the glow-worms are
very still, but we make a prodigious clatter. What does
it matter? It is good for these yokels to be waked up.
Tootle-toot! The diamond-paned lattice of a cottage
flies open. Post-office here. Throw them on their
haunches. Bag up — bag down — and the village has
grown indistinct behind. The old moon is racing us, she
slices through trees like a knife through cheese. Distant
clocks strike midnight. The coach rocks — this is a galloping stage. We have a roan near-wheel and a grey off-
wheel and our leaders are chestnuts, "quick as light,
clever as cats."

The sickle-flame of our lamps cuts past sequences of
trees and well-plashed quickset hedges — hedges of
England, long shafts of the nimbus of London. Hurdles
here and there. Park palings. Reflections in windows.
On — on — through the night to the North. Over
stretched roads, with a soft, continuous motion like
slipping water. Nights and days unwinding down long
roads.

In the green dawn, spires and bell-towers start up and stare at us. Hoary old woods nod and beckon. A castle turret glitters through trees. There is a perfume of wild-rose and honey-bine, twining in the hedges — Northerly hedges, sliding away behind us. The pole-chains tinkle tunes and play a saraband with sheep-bells beyond the hedges. Wedges of fields — square, flat, slatted green with corn, purple with cabbages. The stable clocks of Gayhurst and Tyringham chime from either side of the road. The Ouse twinkles blue among smooth meadows. Go! Go! News of the World! Perhaps a victory! the "Nile" or "Salamanca"! Perhaps a proclamation, or a fall in the rate of consols. Whatever it is, the hedges of England hear it first. Hear it, and flick and flutter their leaves, and catch the dust of it on their shining backs. Bear it over the dumpling hills and the hump-backed bridges. Start it down the rivers: Eden, Eshe, Sark, Milk, Driff, and Clyde. Shout it to the sculptured corbels of old churches. Lurch round corners with it, and stop with a snap before the claret-coloured brick front of the *Bell* at Derby, and call it to the ostler as he runs out with fresh horses. The twenty Corinthian columns of pale primrose alabaster at Keddleston Hall tremble with its importance. Even the runaway couples bound for Gretna Green cheer and wave. Laurels, and ribbons, and a red flag on our roof. "Wellesley forever!"

Dust dims the hedges. A light travelling chariot running sixteen miles an hour with four blood mares doing their bravest. Whip, bound, and cut again. Loose rein, quick spur. He stands up in the chariot and shakes a bag full of broad guineas, you can hear them — clinking, chinking — even above the roar of wheels. "Go it! Go it! We are getting away from them. Fifty guineas to each of you if we get there in time." Quietly wait, grey hedges, it will all happen again: quick whip, spur, strain. Two purple-faced gentlemen in another chariot, black geldings smoking hot, blood and froth flipped over the hedges. They hail the coach: "How far ahead? Can we catch them?" "Ten minutes gone by. Not more." The post-boys wale their lunging horses. Rattle, reel, and plunge.

But the runaways have Jack Ainslee from the *Bush*, Carlisle. He rides in a yellow jacket, and he knows every by-lane and wood between here and the border. In an hour he will have them at Gretna, and to-night the lady will write to her family at Doncaster, and the down mail will carry the letter, with tenpence halfpenny to pay for news that nobody wishes to hear.

"Buy a pottle of plums, Good Sir." "Cherries, fine, ripe cherries O." Get your plums and cherries, and hurry into the *White Horse Cellar* for a last rum and milk. You are a poet, bound to Dover over Westminster Bridge. Ah, well, all the same. You are an Essex

farmer, grown fat by selling your peas at Covent Garden
Market at four guineas a pint. Certainly; as you please.
You are a prebend of Exeter or Wells, timing your jour-
ney to the Cathedral Close. If you choose. You are a
Corinthian Buck going down to Brighton by the *Age*
which runs "with a fury." Mercury on a box seat.

Get up, beavers and top-boots. Shoot the last parcel
in. Now — "Let 'em go. I have 'em." That *was* a jerk,
but the coachman lets fly his whip and quirks his off-
wheeler on the thigh. Out and under the archway of
the coach-yard, with the guard playing "Sally in our
Alley" on his key-bugle. White with sun, the streets of
London. Cloud-shadows run ahead of us along the
streets. Morning. Summer. England. "Have a light,
Sir? Tobacco tastes well in this fresh air."

Hedges of England, how many wheels spatter you in
a day? How many coaches roll between you on their
star-point way? What rainbow colours slide past you
with the fluency of water? Crimson mails rumble and
glide the night through, but the Cambridge *Telegraph*
is a brilliant blue. The *Bull and Mouth* coaches are
buttercup yellow, those of the *Bull* are painted red,
while the *Bell and Crown* sports a dark maroon with
light red wheels. They whirl by in a flurry of dust and
colours. Soon all this will drop asunder like the broken
glass of a kaleidoscope. Hedges, you will see other pictures. New colours will flow beside you. New shapes

will intersect you. Tut! Tut! Have you not hawthorn
blossoms and the hips and haws of roses?

Trundle between your sharp-shorn hedges, old *Tally-
hoes*, and *Comets*, and *Regents*. Stop at the *George*, and
turn with a flourish into the yard, where a strapper is
washing a mud-splashed chaise, and the horsekeeper is
putting a "point" on that best whip of yours. "Coach
stops here half an hour, Gentlemen: dinner quite ready."
A long oak corridor. Then a burst of sunshine through
leaded windows, spangling a floor, iris-tinting rounds of
beef, and flaked veal pies, and rose-marbled hams, and
great succulent cheeses. Wine-glasses take it and break
it, and it quivers away over the table-cloth in faint
rainbows; or, straight and sudden, stamps a startling
silver whorl on the polished side of a teapot of hot bohea.
A tortoise-shell cat naps between red geraniums, and
myrtle sprigs tap the stuccoed wall, gently blowing to
and fro.

Ah, hedges of England, have you led to this? Do
you always conduct to galleried inns, snug bars, beds
hung with flowered chintz, sheets smelling of lav-
ender?

What of the target practice off Spithead? What of
the rocking seventy-fours, flocking like gulls about the
harbour entrances? Hedges of England, can they root
you in the sea?

Your leaves rustle to the quick breeze of wheels inces-

santly turning. This island might be a tread-mill kept
floating right side up by galloping hoofs.

Gabled roofs of *Green Dragons*, and *Catherine Wheels*,
and *Crowns*, ivy-covered walls, cool cellars holding bins
and bins of old port, and claret, and burgundy. You
cannot hear the din of passing chaises, underground,
there is only the sound of beer running into a jug as the
landlord turns the spiggot of a barrel. Green sponge of
England, your heart is red with wine. "Fine spirits and
brandies." Ha! Ha! Good old England, drinking,
blinking, dreading new ideas. Queer, bluff, burly England. You have Nelsons, and Wellesleys, and Tom
Cribbs, but you have also Wordsworths and Rom-
neys, and (a whisper in your ear) Arkwrights and
Stevensons.

"Time's up, Gentlemen; take your places, please!"
The horn rings out, the bars rattle, the horses sidle and
paw and swing; swish — clip — with the long whip, and
away to the hedges again. The high, bordering hedges,
leading to Salisbury, and Bath, and Exeter.

Christmas weather with a hard frost. Hips and haws
sparkle in the hedges, garnets and carnelians scattered
on green baize. The edges of the coachman's hat are
notched with icicles. The horses slip on the frozen
roads. Loads are heavy at this time of year, with rabbits
and pheasants tied under the coach, but it is all hearty

Christmas cheer, rushing between the hedges to get there in time for the plum-pudding. Old England forever! And coach-horns, and waits, and Cathedral organs hail the Star of Bethlehem.

But our star, our London, gutters with fog. The Thames rolls like smoke under charcoal. The dome of St. Paul's is gone, so is the spire of St. Martin's-in-the-Fields, only the fires of torches are brisk and tossing. Tossing torches; tossing heads of horses. Eight mails following each other out of London by torchlight. Scarcely can we see the red flare of the horn lantern in the hand of the ostler at the *Peacock*, but his voice blocks squarely into the fog: "*York Highflyer*," "*Leeds Union*," "*Stamford Regent*." Coach lamps stream and stare, and key-bugles play fugues with each other; "Oh, Dear, What Can the Matter Be?" and "The Flaxen Headed Plough-boy" canon and catch as the mails take the road. There will be no "springing" the horses over the "hospital ground" on a day like this; we cannot make more than three miles an hour in such a fog. Hedges of England, you are only ledges from which water drips back to the sea. The rain is so heavy the coach sways. There will be floods farther on. Floods over the river Mole, with apples, and trees, and hurdles floating. Have a care with your leaders there, they have lost the road, and the wheelers have toppled into a ditch of swirling, curling water. The wheelers flounder and squeal and drown, but the coach is hung up on the stump of a willow-tree, and the passengers have only a broken leg or two among them.

Double thong your team, Coachman, that creaking gibbet on the top of Hindhead is an awesome sight at the fall of night, with the wind roaring and squeaking over the heather. The murder, they say, was done at this spot. Give it to them on the flank, good and hot. "Lord, I wish I had a nip of cherry-brandy." "What was that; down in the bowl!" "Drop my arm, Damn you! or you will roll the coach over!" Teeth chatter, bony castanets — click — click — to a ghastly tune, click — click — on the gallows-tree, where it blows so windily. Blows the caged bones all about, one or two of them have dropped out. The up coach will see them lying on the ground like snow-flakes to-morrow. But we shall be floundering in a drift, and shifting the mail-bags to one of the horses so that the guard can carry them on.

Hedges of England, smothered in snow. Hedges of England, row after row, flat and obliterate down to the sea; but the chains are choked on the gallows-tree. Round about England the toothed waves snarl, gnarling her cliffs of chalk and marl. Crabbed England, consuming beef and pudding, and pouring down magnums of port, to cheat the elements. Go it, England, you will beat Bonaparte yet. What have you to do with ideas!

You have Bishops, and Squires, and Manor-houses, and
— rum.

London shakes with bells. Loud, bright bells clashing over roofs and steeples, exploding in the sunlight
with the brilliance of rockets. Every clock-tower drips
a tune. The people are merry-making, for this is the
King's Birthday and the mails parade this afternoon.

"Messrs. Vidler and Parrat request the pleasure of
Mr. Chaplin's company on Thursday the twenty-eighth
of May, to a cold collation at three o'clock and to see the
Procession of the Mails."

What a magnificent spectacle! A coil of coaches progressing round and round Lincoln's Inn Fields. Sun-
mottled harness, gold and scarlet guards, horns throwing off sprays of light and music. Liverpool, Manchester
— blacks and greys; Bristol, Devonport — satin bays;
Holyhead — chestnuts; Halifax — roans, blue-specked,
rose-specked . . . On their box-seat thrones sit the
mighty coachmen, twisting their horses this way and
that with a turn of the wrist. These are the spokes of a
wheeling sun, these are the rays of London's aureole.
This is her star-fire, reduced by a prism to separate
sparks. Cheer, good people! Chuck up your hats, and
buy violets to pin in your coats. You shall see it all to-
night, when the King's arms shine in lamps from every
house-front, and the mails, done parading, crack their
whips and depart. England forever! Hurrah!

England forever — going to the Prize Fight on Copthorne Common. England forever, with a blue coat and scarlet lining hanging over the back of the tilbury. England driving a gig and one horse; England set up with a curricle and two. England in donkey-carts and coaches. England swearing, pushing, drinking, happy, off to see the "Game Chicken" punch the "Nonpareil's" face to a black-and-blue jelly. Good old England, drunk as a lord, cursing the turn-pike men. Your hedges will be a nest of broken bottles before night, and clouds of dust will quench the perfume of your flowers. I bet you three bulls to a tanner you can't smell a rose for a week.

They've got the soldiers out farther along. "Damn the soldiers! Drive through them, Watson." A fine, manly business; are we slaves? "Britons never — never —" Waves lap the shores of England, waves like watchdogs growling; and long hedges bind her like a bundle. Sit safe, England, trussed and knotted; while your strings hold, all will be well.

But in the distance there is a puff of steam. Just a puff, but it will do. Post-boys, coachmen, guards, chaises, melt like meadow rime before the sun.

You spun your webs over England, hedge to hedge. You kept England bound together by your spinning wheels. But it is gone. They have driven a wedge of iron into your heart. They have dried up the sea, and made pathways in the swimming air. They have tapped the barrels in your cellars and your throats are parched and bleeding. But still the hedges blow for the Spring, and dusty soldiers smell your roses as they tramp to Aldershot or Dorchester.

England forever! Star-pointed and shining. Flinging her hedges out and asunder to embrace the world.

FOUR SIDES TO A HOUSE

PETER, Peter, along the ground,
Is it wind I hear, or your shoes' sound?
Peter, Peter, across the air,
Do dead leaves fall, or is it your hair?
Peter, Peter, North and South,
They have stopped your mouth
With water, Peter.

The long road runs, and the long road runs,
   Who comes over the long road, Peter?
Who knocks at the door in the cold twilight,
And begs a heap of straw for the night,
And a bit of a sup, and a bit of a bite —
   Do you know the face, Peter?

He lays him down on the floor and sleeps.
   Must you wind the clock, Peter?
It will strike and strike the dark night through.
He will sleep past one, he will sleep past two,
But when it strikes three what will he do?
   He will rise and kill you, Peter.

He will open the door to one without.
   Do you hear that voice, Peter?
Two men prying and poking about,

Is it here, is it there, is it in, is it out?
Cover his staring eyes with a clout.
   But you're dead, dead, Peter.

They have ripped up the boards, they have pried up
      the stones,
   They have found your gold, dead Peter.
Ripe, red coins to itch a thief's hand,
But you drip ripe red on the floor's white sand,
You burn their eyes like a firebrand.
   They must quench you, Peter.

It is dark in the North, it is dark in the South.
   The wind blows your white hair, Peter.
One at your feet and one at your head.
A soft bed, a smooth bed,
Scarcely a splash, you sink like lead.
   Sweet water in your well, Peter.

Along the road and along the road,
   The next house, Peter.
Four-square to the bright and the shade of the moor
The North winds shuffle, the South winds croon,
Water with white hair over-strewn.
   The door, the door, Peter!
Water seeps under the door.

   They have risen up in the morning grey.

What will they give to Peter?
The sorrel horse with the tail of gold,
Fastest pacer ever was foaled.
Shoot him, skin him, blanch his bones,
Nail up his skull with a silver nail
Over the door, it will not fail.
No ghostly thing can ever prevail
    Against a horse's skull, Peter.

Over the lilacs, gazing down,
    Is a window, Peter.
The North winds call, and the South winds cry.
Silver white hair in a bitter blowing,
Eel-green water washing by,
A red mouth floating and flowing.
    Do you come, Peter?

They rose as the last star sank and set.
    One more for Peter.
They slew the black mare at the flush of the sun,
And nailed her skull to the window-stone.
In the light of the moon how white it shone —
    And your breathing mouth, Peter!

Around the house, and around the house,
With a wind that is North, and a wind that is South,
    Peter, Peter.

Mud and ooze and a dead man's wrist
Wrenching the shutters apart, like mist
The mud and the ooze and the dead man twist.
    They are praying, Peter.

Three in stable a week ago.
    This is the last, Peter.
"My strawberry roan in the morning clear,
Lady heart and attentive ear,
Foot like a kitten, nose like a deer,
But the fear! The fear!"
    Three skulls, Peter.

The sun goes down, and the night draws in.
    Toward the hills, Peter.
What lies so stiff on the hill-room floor,
When the gusty wind claps to the door?
They have paid three horses and two men more.
    Gather your gold, Peter.

Softly, softly, along the ground
Lest your shoes sound.
Gently, gently, across the air
Lest it stream, your hair,
North and South
For your aching mouth.
But the moon is old, Peter,
And death is long, and the well is deep.
Can you sleep, sleep, Peter?

MEMORANDUM CONFIDED BY A
YUCCA TO A PASSION-VINE

THE Turkey-buzzard was chatting with the Condor
High up in the White Cordillera.
"Surely our friend the fox is mad," said he.
"He chases birds no more and his tail trails lan-
     guidly
Behind him in the dust.
Why, he got it full of cactus-spines one day,
Pawing over a plant that stood in his way.
All the bees are buzzing about it.
Consider a fox who passes by the great hives of sharp,
     black honey
And looks at them no more than a heron would."
"Odd," said the Condor. "Remarkably peculiar."
And he flapped his wings and flew away to the porcelain
     peaks of the distant Sierra.
So the Turkey-buzzard thought no more of the matter,
But busied himself with the carcass of a dead llama.

And the sun boomed onward over the ice-peaks:
Hot — Hot — Hotter!
And the sun dropped behind the snow-peaks,

And the cool of shadow was so delicious that all the
    squirrels and rabbits and peccaries and lizards
Flirted their tails;
And the flamingoes in Lake Titicaca puffed out their
    gizzards,
And waded into the pink water reflected from the
    carmine-tinted mountain summits;
And the parrots chattered and flashed in the mimosas;
And the eagles dove like plummets
Upon the unfortunate alpacas.
The animals were enjoying themselves in the rose-red
    light that lingers
Flung from the blood-orchid tips of the mountains
Before the night mists slide over the foothills.
Ah! But you could see them in the valleys,
Floating and circling like dead men's fingers
Combing living hair.

In a place of bright quartz rocks,
Sits a small red fox.
He is half in the shade of a cactus-bush.
The birds still fly, but there is a hush
And a sifting of purple through the air:
Blue dims rose,
The evening is fair.
Why is the red fox waiting there,
With his sniffing nose,
And his stiffened pose,

And his narrow eyelids which never close?
"Fox — fox —
Against the rocks.
Are you rooted there till the equinox?"
So the alcamarines flocking home in the afterglow
Mock the poor fox, but he doesn't seem to know.
He sits on his haunches, staring high
Into the soft, fruit-green evening sky.

A yellow rose blooms in the glow,
Thin fox frosted by silver snow,
Mica-crystals flecking over indigo.
And a cactus-tree
Grating its thorn-leaves huskily.
Moan of wind and the crackles of an empty place
At the coming of night.
The fox is alone.
Then in the far green heavens the lady rises, tall and
      white.
August and dazzling
In the drooping light,
She shimmers, jubilantly bright.
Breasts and thighs tuned to liquid air,
Loveliness set naked in a firmament.
He sees the slim, smooth arms,
And the virgin waist bending with delicate movement.
Her body sways as a flower stem
Caught in a gust;

And her hair is thrust
Towards him, he can see the gem
Which binds it loosely. His eyes are greedy
Of the curving undulations and straight fall
Following down from head to foot, and all
Cool and unclouded, touching him almost.
With hot tongue he pants upon the splendour
Of this marble beauty, imperious and unashamed
In her extreme of excellence.
Then he weeps,
Weeps in little yelping barks for the cold beautiful
   body
Of the inaccessible moon.
The villagers wake in a startled fright
And tell each other: "A fox bays the moon to-night."

The moon lives in Cuzco —
It was the Partridge who told him so —
In a temple builded of jointured stone
On an emerald-studded, silver throne.
So the fox set out for Cuzco with his tail held high to
   keep it out of the dust.

Tramp! Tramp! Tramp!
What is that noise approaching him?
Quick, behind a stone,
And he watches them come,
The soldiers of the great Inca.

Copper spear-heads running like a river of gold along
    the road.
Helmets of tiger-skins, coats of glittering feathers,
A ripple of colours from one edge of the way to the
    other.
Feet of men cadenced to the swing of weapons.
So many bows, and arrows, and slings, and darts, and
    lances,
A twinkling rhythm of reflections to which the army
    advances,
And a rainbow banner flickering colours to the slipping
    of the wind.
They pass as water passes and the fox is left behind.
"Those men come from Cuzco," thought the fox,
And his heart was like lead in his stomach for wonder-
    ing if they knew the moon.
Then he trotted on again with his tail held high to
    keep it out of the dust.

Pat! Pat! Pat!
What is that sound behind him?
He leaps into a bush of tufted acacia just in time.
It is a post-runner, doing his stint of five miles,
Carrying merchandise from the coast.
And the fox's mouth waters as he smells fish:
Bobos, shads, sardines,
All fading in a little osier basket,
Faint colours whispering the hues of the rainbow flag.

But the runner must not lag,
These fish are for the Inca's table.
A flash of feet against the heart-shaped flowers of the
     yolosuchil
And the jarred leaves settle and are still.
The fox creeps out and resumes his journey, with his
     tail held high to keep it out of the dust.

Over bush and bramble and prick and thorn
Goes the fox, till his feet are torn,
And his eyes are weary with keeping the trail
Through ashen wind and clattering hail,
With the hot, round sun lying flat on his head,
And morning crushing its weight of lead
On scores of trumpet-vines tangled and dead.
Across swung bridges of plaited reeds
In a whorl of foaming, bursting beads
Of river mist, where a cañon makes a fall
Of thousands of feet in a sheer rock wall.
Pomegranates toss him scarlet petals,
The little covetous claws of nettles
Catch at his fur, and a sudden gloom
Blocks his path on a drip of bloom.
Over prick and thorn and bush and bramble;
Up pointed boulders with a slip and scramble,
Past geese with flattened, blue-green wings
Pulling the ichu grass which springs
In narrow fissures where nothing else clings;

Through terraced fields of bright-tongued maize
Licking the hills to a golden blaze;
Under clustered bananas and scented oaks;
Across dry, high plains where the yucca chokes.
Dawns explode in bleeding lights
On the snow-still uplands of ghastly heights
Where long-dead bodies stare through their hair
Crooking their brittle legs and bare
Ice-tortured arms, and the sun at noon
Is a glassy shell of dull maroon.
Only at night he watches the moon
Stepping along the smooth, pale sky
In a silver florescence. By and by
The red fox reaches the gates of Cuzco,
But his tail is very much bedraggled for he can
        no longer hold it up out of the dust.

Morning playing dimly in the passion-vines
Hanging over the gates of Cuzco.
Morning picking out a purple flower —
Another — another —
Cascading down the walls of Cuzco.
Scarlet-flashing, uprose the sun
With one deep bell-note of a copper-crashed gong.
Glory of rose-mist over the Sierra,
Glory of crimson on the tinted turrets
Of the wide old fort under the high cliff.
Glory of vermilion dripping from the windows,

Glory of saffron streaking all the shadows,
House fronts glaring in fresh young light,
Gold over Cuzco!
Gold!
Gold!
In an orchid flow,
Where the Temple of Pachacamac rose like a bell
Shining on the city,
With the clear sweet swell of an open sunrise gong.
White and carnation,
White and carnation,
The sun's great gnomon,
Measuring its shadow on the long sharp gold polished
      grass.
Who pass here
In an early year?
Lightning and Thunder,
Servants of the Sun.
Lord of the rainbow's white and purple,
Blue and carnation,
All awhirl to a curl of gold.
He who comes from the land of monkeys,
He who comes from the flying-fishes playing games with
      rainbow dolphins,
Pause —
Here before the gates of gold.
Chamfered crown about the Temple,
Sparkling points and twisted spirals,

All of Gold.
Lemon-tinted Gold,
Red-washed fire Gold,
Gold, the planking,
Gold, the roof-tree,
Gold the burnished doors and porches,
And the chairs of the dead Incas.
One long row of stately bodies
Sitting dead in all the dazzle
Glittering with bright green emeralds.
White-haired Incas,
Hoary Incas,
Black and shiny-haired young Incas,
All dead Incas;
With their hands crossed on their breasts
And their eyes cast down, they wait there.
Terrible and full-fleshed Incas.
Blaze of fire, burning, glaring,
Bright, too bright!
Ah-h-h!
The Sun!
Up through the wide-open Eastern portal,
Broken, sharpened on a thousand plates of gold,
It falls,
Splintered into prisms on the rainbow walls,
The Sun steps into his house.
Hush! It is the PRESENCE!
Face of Pachacamac,

Wreathed in burnished flames of swift fire.
Then on the wind of a thousand voices rises the
      hymn:
           "Pachacamac
           World's Creator,
           Mountain-mover,
           Heaven-dwelling.
           We beseech thee
           Send thy showers,
           Warm our meadows,
           Bless the seed-ears.
           Man and woman,
           Beast and lizard,
           Feathered people,
           Whales and fishes,
           All implore thee,
           Clement God-head,
           To make fruitful
           These thy creatures.
           String their sinews
           Ripe for power,
           Quicken wombs and
           Eggs and rootlets.
           Be the Father,
           The Begetter.
           Pour upon us,
           Lord of all things,
           Of thy bounty,

Of thy fulness.
So we praise thee,
Swelling Apple,
Gourd of Promise,
Mighty Melon,
Seed-encaser,
Sun and Spirit,
Lord of Morning,
Blood of Mercy,
Pachacamac!"

And the great tide of men's voices echoed and curved
    upon the plates of gold
Lining the Temple
So that it became a wide horn of melody,
And out of it burst the hymn like a red-streaked lily
    thundering to the morning.
Men's voices singing the hymn of ripening seed,
Men's voices raised in a phallic chorus to the rising
    sun . . .
Virgin of the Sun,
Pale Virgin,
Through the twisting vine-leaves it comes to you broken
    and shivering.
What are you, Virgin?
And who is this all-wise God
That shuts you in a hall of stone?
Cleft asunder,
A white pomegranate with no seeds,

A peascod dropped on a foot-path before its peas are
    blown.
Pale Virgin, go about your baking,
For the shadows shorten and at noon the oven will be
    heated.

Tired little fox outside the fence,
Lie down in the shade of the wall,
For indeed the sun has done you an injury.

Now the East wind, called Brisa, blew against the
    clouds;
And the sun rushed up the sky;
And at noon the shadow of the great gnomon was not,
No single dark patch lay anywhere about its foot,
For the God sat with all his light upon the column.
The fox awoke, and sought shelter from the heat.
Creeping, he came to a garden of five fountains,
Set in green plots, and plots of silver.
For there he saw, mixed, the fruits of the sun:
Apples, quinces, loquats, and chirimoyas,
All just after flowering with their fruit-balls perfectly
    formed but each smaller than a pepper-grain,
And the fruits of man:
Oranges, melons, cocoanuts and breadfruit,
Fashioned of gold and silver,
Amazing with brightness.
Indian corn sprouted from the earth on thin stalks of gold

Which rattled against one another with a sweet clashing,
The golden ears escaping smartly out of broad recurved
      leaves of silver,
And silver tassels floated in a twinkle of whiteness from
      their glittering tops.
Golden snails clung to silver palm-branches,
Turquoise butterflies flew hither and thither
And one alone remained poised; it was of polished stone.
The fox gaped for wonder and his tail lay prone on a
      silver lizard,
But this he never noticed.
Then across the sounds of leaves blowing
And metals tapping,
Came music;
A voice singing in a minor key,
Throaty and uncertain as a new-cut reed.
"Mama Quilla," it sang.
"Mother Moon,
Through the shell of heaven gliding.
Moon of many stars and brothers,
Mistress of the bright-haired rainbow,
Wife and sister of the Sun-god,
Virgin moon who bore him children,
If you die then do we perish.
Mama Quilla,
I, a Virgin,
Crave a blessing,
Ask a guerdon.

O glorious, chaste, and immaculate moon,
Preserve me to my vows.
But, I implore thee,
Take from me, therefore, this my longing,
Let the Spring deal with me gently,
Still my spirit.
Or, devout and pitying mother,
Give me thunder,
Give me lightning,
Break me on a green-stone anvil,
So the flower of my body
Blow to loveliness a moment.
I am past my holding, Mama Quilla,
In the night I smell the strong-scented blossoms of the
          daturas,
And my heart snares me in its loneliness."

So the fox crept up to the door where the Virgin of the
          Sun sat spinning.
"Can you tell me, Lady," said he, making a fine bow,
"If the moon lives here in Cuzco?"
Then the Virgin was afraid,
For she did not know that foxes spoke.
"Who are you," she demanded,
"And whence do you come?"
"I am a fox of the Western Country,
And I come from the water-passage of Lake Titicaca.
I love the moon,

I desire her more than the monkeys of the Eastern
    forests
Desire dates,
More than your kinsmen, the Incas,
Desire the land of the Machigangas.
She is more beautiful to me than red pepper-pods
To the shepherds who walk the mountains with their
    llamas.
I prize her more greatly than do the Aquarimas the
    shrunken skulls of their enemies.
She is a poison-tree of many branches:
With one, she brushes the waves of the ocean
So that all the shores are overflown with the sea at
    Spring tides;
And, with another, she tickles the nose of a tapir
Asleep in a grove of vanilla-trees
On the banks of the Amazon;
And I have been blinded by the sweeping of a third
Above the snow-cornice on Mount Vilcanota.
Oh, she has many branches
All dripping with silver-white poison,
And I have come here to drink this poison and die."
"But you cannot possess the moon;
It is sacrilege," cried the Virgin,
And her hands trembled so that the distaff fell to the
    ground.
"And it is sacrilege for a Virgin of the Sun to sing of the
    labours of women," said the fox.

Then the fox told of his watching, night and night,
      under the cactus-bush,
Of his great pains and hungering,
And the Virgin listened in a tiptoe of attention,
While the ruby humming-birds splashed fire across the
      silver ripple of the garden,
And the fountains sprang and recoiled,
And the Sun sank behind the mountains of the sea.

Hush!
Hush!
In the House of Acllahua.
The Mamacunas sleep,
The Virgins lie enmeshed in sleep.
Sleep folded on the House of Acllahua,
While the Sun, their master,
Dries the ocean with his swimming.
West to East, all night he swims,
And they in the House of Acllahua sleep.
Only she is waiting, fearing;
Now more gently, gently, gliding,
Through the fluttering silver flowers.
And the fox is waiting,
Sitting under a tamarisk-tree
With his hot tongue hanging out of his mouth.
Through the thin cloud of tamarisk-leaves
Falls a tempered moonlight,
A feathered, partial moonlight,

A moonlight growing every moment stronger,
A shadow growing every minute blacker.
The Virgin and the fox under the black feathers of the
    tamarisk-tree,
While the moon walks with a stately slowness
Down the long, quiet terraces of the sky.
Hush!
Hush!
The garden burns with cold, green fire,
A bat spots black on a gold sweet-briar,
A polished rose on a stem of wire
Sweeps and bends, a blue flung ball
Palpitating,
Undulating,
All the trees and plants girating,
All the metals quivering to song
And the great palmettos beating gongs.
The low, slow notes of the water-reeds
Underscore the glass-sweet beads
Of the little clapping melon seeds.
Gold and silver strings of a lyre
Plucked by the wind, high pitched and higher,
And the silver moans with a tone of its own
Fragile as an ixia newly blown.
All the garden sways to a noise
Of humming metal in equipoise.
Stately dates sweep a merry-go-round,
The fountains spring in a sparkle of sound.

The moonlight falls in a heap on the ground.
And there is Light!
Light in a crowned effulgence
Thrown up from the flowers and trees,
Delicate, pearled light, barred by beautiful shadows,
Bloomed light, plunging upon the silver-roofed Temple.
Open, Open,
Door of the Temple of the Moon.
Come forth, dead mothers of dead Incas.
Slow procession of the dead
Filing out of the Temple.
Mama Vello, mother of Huayna Capac,
Mama Runtu,
Mama Ocllo.
Feathered mantles brush the golden gravel,
Their hands are crossed on their breasts,
They are powdered with turquoises and raw-cut
    emeralds.
Slowly the Inca mothers form a ring,
They hold a golden chain
Long and broad as the great street of Cuzco.
Slowly they move in a circle,
Chanting.
Their steps are soft as weeping water.
Their voices are faint as snow dropping through
    Autumn dusk.
Suddenly, in the midst of the ring, a great fall of
    Light.

It is she — the MOON!
White mist circumvolves about her,
On her head is a diadem of opal-changing ice,
And hoar-frost follows the stepping of her feet.
A single emerald, half white, half foaming green,
Clasps a girdle about her waist.
Terribly she dances in the ring of Inca mothers.
The garden turns with them as they move,
Winding and closing about them,
Impelling them toward the Temple,
Up to the Altar.
Trumpets, brazen and vainglorious,
Silver-striking, shouting cymbals,
Open horns, round gourd-drums beaten to a rattle of
        flame.
Movement, ghostly, perpetual,
And sound, loud, sweet, sucking from the four edges of
        the sky.
Everything swings, and sings, and oscillates, and curves.
Only the moon upon the High Altar is still.
She stands, struck to immobility,
Then, without haste, unclasps the foaming emerald
And the mists part and fall . . .
Silence —
Silence spread beneath her as a footstool.
The flowers close;
The Inca mothers are dead corpses on their silver
        thrones.

But She!
Naked, white, and beautiful,
Poised and infinite;
Flesh,
Spirit,
Woman and Unparalleled Enchantment.
Moon of waters,
Womb of peoples,
Majesty and highest Queen.
So the Goddess burns in a halo of white-rose fire
For an instant . . .
Yelp! Yelp! Yelp!
The fox has burst from the Virgin's grasp.
Over the garden,
Up the aisle of the Temple,
With staring eyes
And ghoulish, licking tongue.
Satyr fox assaulting the moon!
THUNDER!!!
Lightning serpents
Wound in great circles above the Temple.
Sheets of lightning snarling from racing, purple clouds
And rain roaring down the hot walls of a copper sky.

The clouds splinter, and a ruined moon wavers up into
        the heavens, about her are three great rings, one
        of blood, one of black, and the utmost all of
        stinging, glutinous, intorting coils of smoke.

Upon the disk of the moon are spots, black obscene
  spots, the print of a fox's paws.

* * * * * *

Bake your cakes of the sacred maize, Virgin,
Tend the flame the priest has gathered with his metal
  sun-glass,
Weave feathered mantles for the Coya,
Burn holy gums to deaden the scent of the daturas.
If you and the moon have a secret,
Let it rest there.

FOOL O' THE MOON

THE silver-slippered moon treads the blue tiles
     of the sky,
And I
See her dressed in golden roses,
With a single breast uncovered,
The carnation tip of it
Urgent for a lover's lip.
So she dances to a stately
Beat, with poses most sedately
Taken, yet there lies
Something wanton in her gestures,
And there is surprise of coquetry
In the falling of her vestures.
Why?

Out of old mythology,
With a pulse of gourds and sheep-skins,
Banging bronze and metal thunders,
There is she,
Wonderfullest of earth's wonders.
As for me,
Head thrown back and arms spread wide

Like a zany crucified,
I stand watching, waiting, gazing,
All of me spent in amazing,
Longing for her wheat-white thighs,
Thirsting for her emerald fire,
My desire
Pounding dully from my eyes.
And my hands
Clutch and cuddle the vast air
Seeking her where she's most fair.

There,
On the cool blue tiles of heaven,
She is dancing coolly, coldly,
Footsteps trace a braid of seven,
And her gauzy garments fleet
Round her like a glittering sleet.
Suddenly she flings them boldly
In a streaming bannerall
Out behind,
And I see all.
God! I'm blind!

And a goodly company
Of men are we,
Lovers she has chosen,
Laughing-stocks and finger-posts
To the wise, a troupe of ghosts

Swelled by every century.
Mad, and blind, and burnt, and frozen,
Standing on a hilly slope
At bright midnight,
And our hope
Is in vain, or is it not?
Legend knows the very spot
Where the moon once made her bed.
But the pathway as it led
Over rock-brows to that valley
Is an alley choked and dead.
One by one our fates deceive us,
One of hundreds will be shown
Ferny uplands whose great bosses
Of tall granite hide the mosses
Where our Lady's lying prone,
All her stars withdrawn, alone.
So she chooses to receive us,
Out of hundreds, only one.

Such a vale of moss and heather
Spreads about us, hither — thither.
Hush!
Shall I tell what befell
Once behind that bush.
When the rattling pods at noon
Made a music in September.
Shall I say what I remember —

While the long, sea-grasses croon,
And the sea-spray on the sand
Chips the silence from the land?
Hush, then, let me say it soon.
I have lain with Mistress Moon.

WIND AND SILVER

GREATLY shining,
The Autumn moon floats in the thin sky;
And the fish-ponds shake their backs and flash their
      dragon scales
As she passes over them.

LACQUER PRINTS AND CHINOISERIES

PROPORTION

IN the sky there is a moon and stars,
And in my garden there are yellow moths
Fluttering about a white azalea bush.

HOAR-FROST

IN the cloud-grey mornings
I heard the herons flying;
And when I came into my garden,
My silken outer-garment
Trailed over withered leaves.
A dried leaf crumbles at a touch,
But I have seen many Autumns
With herons blowing like smoke
Across the sky.

DESOLATION

UNDER the plum-blossoms are nightingales;
But the sea is hidden in an egg-white mist,
And they are silent.

THE POND

COLD, wet leaves
Floating on moss-coloured water,
And the croaking of frogs —
Cracked bell-notes in the twilight.

A BURNT OFFERING

BECAUSE there was no wind,
The smoke of your letters hung in the air
For a long time;
And its shape
Was the shape of your face,
My Beloved.

THE FISHERMAN'S WIFE

WHEN I am alone,
The wind in the pine-trees
Is like the shuffling of waves
Upon the wooden sides of a boat.

SPRING LONGING

THE South wind blows open the folds of my dress,
My feet leave wet tracks in the earth of my garden,
The willows along the canal sing
          with new leaves turned upon the wind.

I walk along the tow-path
Gazing at the level water.

Should I see a ribbed edge
Running upon its clearness,
I should know that this was caused
By the prow of the boat
In which you are to return.

ONE OF THE "HUNDRED VIEWS OF FUJI" BY HOKUSAI

BEING thirsty,
I filled a cup with water,
And, behold! Fuji-yama lay upon the water
Like a dropped leaf!

PEACE

PERCHED upon the muzzle of a cannon
A yellow butterfly is slowly opening and shutting
    its wings.

FROM A LEGEND OF PORCELAIN

BEAUTIFUL the sun of China,
Beautiful the squares of flooded rice-fields,
The long slopes of tea plants on the hills of Ning-po,
The grey mulberry-trees of Chuki.
Beautiful the cities between the rivers,
But three, and three, and three times more beautiful
The porcelains fashioned by Chou-Kiou.
See them in the sun,
Swept over by the blowing shade of willows,
Moulded like lotus-leaves,
Yellow as the skins of eels,
Black glaze overlaid with gold.
Tell the story of this porcelain
With veins like arbor-vitæ leaves and bullock's hair,
Mottled as hare's fur,
Bright and various as the wooded walls of mountains.
Here are the dawn-red wine-cups,
And the cups of snow-blue with no glisten;
Little vases, barely taller than a toad,
And great, three-part vases shining slowly like tarnished
　　　　silver.
They stand in rows along the flat board

And she checks them, one by one, on a tablet of fir-
    flower paper,
And her eyes are little copper bells fallen in the midst of
    tall grass.
Tell the tale of these great jars,
Cloudy coloured as the crystal grape
With white bloom of rice-dust upon them,
Fallen over at the top by pointed bunches
Of the myriad-year wistaria.
Those smaller jars of moonlight enamel, dark and pale,
With undulating lines which seem to change.
Pots green as growing plants are green,
Marked with the hundred-fold crackle of broken ice.
Pallets painted blue with dragons,
And ample dishes, redder than fresh blood,
Spotted with crabs' claws,
Splashed with bluish flames of fire.
Here are bowls faintly tinted as tea-dust
Or the fading leaf of the camphor-tree in Autumn;
Others as bamboo paper for thickness,
Lightly spattered with vermilion fishes;
And white bowls
Surpassing hoar-frost and the pointed tips of icicles.
There are birds painted thinly in dull reds,
Fighting-cocks with rose-pink legs and crests of silver,
Teapots rough as the skin of the Kio orange, or blistered
    with the little flower-buds of the Tsong-tree.
How tell the carminates,

The greens of pale copper,
The leopard-spotted yellows,
The blues, powdered and indefinite as a Mei plum!
Globular bodies with bulbous mouths;
Slim, long porcelains confused like a weedy sea;
Porcelains, pale as the morning sky
Fluttered with purple wings of finches;
High-footed cups for green wine,
And incense-burners yellow as old Llama books
With cranes upon them.
Blue porcelain for the Altar of Heaven,
Yellow for the Altar of Earth,
Red for the Altar of the Sun,
White for the Altar of the Year-star.
All these Chou-Kiou sets down on her fir-flower tablet,
Then carefully, carefully, selects a cup
Of so keen a transparence that the sun, passing it, can
        scarcely mark a shadow,
And fills it with water.
Oh! The purple fishes!
The dark-coloured fishes with scales of silver!
The blue-black fishes swerving in a trail of gold!
They move and flicker,
They swing in procession,
They dart, and hesitate, and float
With flower-waving tails —
The vase is empty again,
Smooth and open and colourless.

The tally is finished,
The sun is sinking in a rose-green sky,
And in the guard-house down the road
The red tallow candles are lighted.

THE THATCHED HOUSE UNROOFED BY AN AUTUMN GALE

BY TU FU

IT is the Eighth Month, the very height of Autumn.

The wind rages and roars.

It tears off three layers of my grass-roof.

The thatch flies — it crosses the river — it is scattered about in the open spaces by the river.

High-flying, it hangs, tangled and floating, from the tops of forest trees;

Low-flying, it whirls — turns — and sinks into the hollows of the marsh.

The swarm of small boys from the South Village laugh at me because I am old and feeble.

How dare they act like thieves and robbers before my face,

Openly seizing my thatch and running into my bamboo grove?

My lips are scorched, my mouth dry, I scream at them, but to no purpose.

I return, leaning on my staff. I sigh and breathe heavily.

Presently, of a sudden, the wind ceases. The clouds are the colour of ink.

The Autumn sky is endless — endless — stretching toward dusk and night.

My old cotton quilt is as cold as iron;

My restless son sleeps a troubled sleep, his moving foot tears the quilt.

Over the head of the bed is a leak. Not a place is dry.

The rain streams and stands like hemp — there is no break in its falling.

Since this misery and confusion, I have scarcely slept or dozed.

All the long night, I am soaking wet. When will the light begin to sift in?

If one could have a great house of one thousand, ten thousand rooms —

A great shelter where all the Empire's shivering scholars could have happy faces —

Not moved by wind or rain, solid as a mountain —

Alas! When shall I see that house standing before my eyes?

Then, although my own hut were destroyed, although I might freeze and die, I should be satisfied.

THE LONELY WIFE

BY LI T'AI-PO

THE mist is thick. On the wide river, the water-plants
     float smoothly.
No letters come; none go.
There is only the moon, shining through the clouds of a
     hard, jade-green sky,
Looking down at us so far divided, so anxiously apart.
All day, going about my affairs, I suffer and grieve, and
     press the thought of you closely to my heart.
My eyebrows are locked in sorrow, I cannot separate
     them.
Nightly, nightly, I keep ready half the quilt,
And wait for the return of that divine dream which is
     my Lord.

Beneath the quilt of the Fire-Bird, on the bed of the
     Silver-Crested Love-Pheasant,
Nightly, nightly, I drowse alone.
The red candles in the silver candlesticks melt, and the
     wax runs from them,
As the tears of your so Unworthy One escape and con-
     tinue constantly to flow.
A flower face endures but a short season,

Yet still he drifts along the river Hsiao and the river
  Hsiang.
As I toss on my pillow, I hear the cold, nostalgic sound
  of the water-clock:
Shêng! Shêng! it drips, cutting my heart in two.

I rise at dawn. In the Hall of Pictures
They come and tell me that the snow-flowers are falling.
The reed-blind is rolled high, and I gaze at the beautiful,
  glittering, primeval snow,
Whitening the distance, confusing the stone steps and
  the courtyard.
The air is filled with its shining, it blows far out like the
  smoke of a furnace.
The grass-blades are cold and white, like jade girdle
  pendants.
Surely the Immortals in Heaven must be crazy with
  wine to cause such disorder,
Seizing the white clouds, crumpling them up, destroying
  them.

DRINKING IN THE T'AO PAVILION

BY LI T'AI-PO

THE house of the lonely scholar is in the winding lane.
The great scholar's gate is very high.
The garden pool lies and shines like the magic gall
    mirror;
Groves of trees throw up flowers with wide, open faces;
The leaf-coloured water draws the Spring sun.
Sitting in the green, covered passage-way, watching the
    strange, red clouds of evening,
Listening to the lovely music of flageolets and strings,
The Golden Valley is not much to boast of.

THE RETREAT OF HSIEH KUNG

BY LI T'AI-PO

THE sun is setting — has set — on the Spring-green
   Mountain.
Hsieh Kung's retreat is solitary and still.
No sound of man in the bamboo grove.
The white moon shines in the centre of the unused gar-
   den pool.
All round the ruined Summer-house is decaying grass,
Grey mosses choke the abandoned well.
There is only the free, clear wind
Again — again — passing over the stones of the spring.

IN DEEP THOUGHT, GAZING AT THE MOON

BY LI T'AI-PO

THE clear spring reflects the thin, wide-spreading pine-
  tree —
And for how many thousand, thousand years?
No one knows.
The late Autumn moon shivers along the little water
  ripples,
The brilliance of it flows in through the window.
Before it I sit for a long time absent-mindedly chanting,
Thinking of my friend —
What deep thoughts!
There is no way to see him. How then can we speak to-
  gether?
Joy is dead. Sorrow is the heart of man.

"RODE THE SIX HUNDRED"

A June-bug has just flown in through my window,
And to-day I sat among narcissus and grape-hyacinths
Drinking the sudden sun.
The terrible Winter has passed
Flinging my garden full of flowers.
But for me I think it will not be long,
Not long,
Before it is the end.

Ah, my flowers!

INDEX BY VOLUMES

INDEX BY VOLUMES

[1] Written in collaboration with Florence Ayscough.